W9-CUE-631

# The *NEW* CREATIVE DIVORCE

# The *NEW* CREATIVE DIVORCE

**How to Create a Happier, More Rewarding Life During–and After–Your Divorce**

MEL KRANTZLER, Ph.D.
& PAT KRANTZLER, M.A.

Adams Media Corporation
HOLBROOK, MASSACHUSETTS

Copyright ©1998, Mel Krantzler and Pat Krantzler. All rights reserved.
This book, or parts thereof, may not be reproduced in any form
without permission from the publisher; exceptions are made
for brief excerpts used in published reviews.

Published by
Adams Media Corporation
260 Center Street, Holbrook, MA 02343

ISBN: 1-58062-054-X

Printed in the United States of America.

J I H G F E D C B A

**Library of Congress Cataloging-in-Publication Data**
Krantzler, Mel.
The new creative divorce / by Mel Krantzler and Pat Krantzler.
p. cm.
Includes index.
ISBN 1-58062-054-X
1. Divorce—United States. 2. Divorced people—United States—Psychology.
I. Krantzler, Patricia B. II. Title.
HQ834.K74 1998
306.89—dc21 98-7601
CIP

Although the events, locales, and personalities in this book are accurate, the names and identifying details of the individuals have been changed in order to protect their privacy.

This publication is designed to provide accurate and authoritative information with regard to the subject matter covered. It is sold with the understanding that the publisher is not engaged in rendering legal, accounting, or other professional advice. If legal advice or other expert assistance is required, the services of a competent professional person should be sought.

— From a *Declaration of Principles* jointly adopted by a Committee of the American Bar Association and a Committee of Publishers and Associations

Cover photo ©Henry Allen\Uniphoto

*This book is available at quantity discounts for bulk purchases.
For information, call 1-800-872-5627 (in Massachusetts, 781-767-8100).*

**Visit our home page at http://www.adamsmedia.com**

# CONTENTS

# INTRODUCTION

In the early 1970s, I was a recently divorced man desperately trying to make sense out of my "new" life. Where to go? What to do? Where were the helping resources for people like me? "Nowhere" was the answer.

Here I was a practicing psychologist experiencing shock and surprise that my own emotions were in total disarray. Instead of the fresh start I expected, I faced chaos. Life for me had always been a twosome affair, since I had married in my early twenties and lived for two decades with a wife and two daughters, now in their teens. Now, however, I was living alone in a shabby one-and-a-half-room apartment with walls so thin that I would catch myself from saying "God bless you" when someone sneezed next door.

I was the first member of my family of origin to be divorced, so here I was wandering aimlessly in an uncharted country. Even shopping in a supermarket was a strange experience. When I was married, I never bothered about whether or not frozen or canned foods came in one-serving portions for one person. But now I looked in vain for that one-person package or can; it seemed even food came in quantities designed for couples. The mathematics were clear: "One" was a zero number.

. . . And zero was how I felt. Continuing education college programs only presented marriage courses, and the few books then published on divorce spoke of the subject as if it were a form of leprosy, implying you were a failure for turning into a single person and could only cure yourself by marrying again as soon as possible.

Pat, the equal partner who created this book (doing the research and editing while I did the writing), felt as confused and hurt as I did when she was divorced. After sixteen years of marriage and with two teenage daughters, she too found herself in this nowhere land of singleness. "I cried every night that first month," she said. "I was living alone, hoping my ex would change his ways so he could come back a new man, and we would live happily ever after as husband and wife. But I also knew that was hopeless. I felt like two persons: the fantasy me who hoped for a movie-story happy ending and the realistic me who now knew that my hope had as much chance of happening as my winning a lottery.

"All of my life I was programmed to believe my sole purpose was to become a wife and mother. That's why I quit college, where women at that time went to find good marriage material. I found my man there—oh so handsome!—quit school, and at the age of twenty-one had two daughters. Instead of good marriage material, my husband turned out to be damaged goods. But I stayed in my marriage sixteen years, because I had believed divorce was inconceivable. Divorce would mean I was nothing. A wife meant status in my community, a divorce meant you were an outcast. I would think of the time when I was eight years old and there was a divorced woman living on our block. I was told not to go near her. It was like she had a disease I could catch. Once I passed her on the street. She smiled at me and said hello. She seemed nice. I looked at her carefully but could see no sign of her divorce disease and wondered where it was located. Since there was no help for divorced women then, all of my friends told me to date immediately so I could marry again as soon as possible and so regain my self-esteem. They meant well, but all they did was scare me off from men, because I was so insecure and couldn't trust my own judgment. What if I were attracted to another damaged goods person?"

When Pat and I met in the early seventies, we shared our confused divorce experiences and found that we were both hurting in many of the same ways: we felt divorce was shameful, a blow to our self-esteem; we had mixed feelings about our ex-spouses; we felt hurt and found our good friends wanting to help us, but they were not really helpful. We both felt "one" was a very lonely number. I have written about our four-year journey from our first meeting two years after each of us was divorced to our courtship and marriage in a previous book entitled *Learning to Love Again*. In that period of time each of us had learned to become separate individuals with a confident sense of self-esteem. And out of that learning experience we decided to get married out of free choice: we *wanted* to marry rather than *needed* to marry because society and our families-of-origin demanded we do so.

During the first year after my divorce, I felt I was suffering from a case of Physician-Heal-Thyself. I began that healing process by deciding that since there were no educational courses available for divorced men and women, I would establish such a course and make it available in the continuing education departments of the colleges in my area, for I was an educator with teaching experience as well as a clinical psychologist. That way I would learn from other divorced people (Am I going crazy? Am I normal? What are all the other divorced persons experiencing?) and they in turn could learn from me.

Because I lived in Northern California, twenty miles north of San Francisco, it was much easier to gain approval for my divorce program in colleges such as San Francisco State and U.C. Berkeley, since they were receptive to what was then an innovative and "strange" program. Strange indeed, for whoever thought a twelve-week program devoted to learning how divorce personally affected people would be possible?

It turned out there were thousands of divorced men and women in my metropolitan area who did not think it was strange at all. My class, which I called Creative Divorce: A New Opportunity for Personal Growth, was oversubscribed every time I gave it, beginning in 1971. I had really touched a nerve—the need of countless numbers of men and women who were walking wounded through the minefields of their divorces.

I can truthfully say I learned as much, if not more, from the men and women in those classes as they learned from me. They gave me the insight to see that I was not alone, that divorce was a universal emotional experience. They taught me that it was absurd to believe that men and women are from different planets; we bleed equally in divorce. They taught me that indeed divorce could be an opportunity for self-renewal and demonstrated that fact by improving their lives as single persons. Indeed, there was life after divorce and the quality of that life could be better than it was in a dead-end relationship. They taught me empathy, compassion, and courage as I saw many of them seize the opportunity to prevail over their severe economic and social difficulties. Indeed, they taught me that instead of vengeance, living well was the best revenge against the cruel actions of their ex-spouses, their lawyers, and their false friends.

I incorporated their personal experiences and my own in my book *Creative Divorce: A New Opportunity for Personal Growth*, the same title as my divorce course. It was published in 1973 and remained in print until July 1996 without a single change in its content. It had a universal appeal. I myself was surprised that the first country to buy foreign rights to my book was Japan! And the second was Finland! All in all, a dozen countries bought foreign rights to my book, and it appeared on the *New York Times* bestseller list for six months. It is the only divorce book that ever sold over three million copies.

The reason why the old *Creative Divorce* remained in print for 23 years was the fact that it was the first to offer hope to the divorced: there really was light at the end of the dark tunnel of despair, and the book charted the way in which divorced men and women could seize the opportunity to move into the light.

However, that book has now outlived its time. Since 1973, we have experienced tumultuous changes in the social, economic, cultural, and religious character of our society, so much so that a Rip Van Winkle who slept through the last twenty-five years would find it hard to believe he was living in the same United States. When he went to sleep in 1973, divorce meant you were a selfish, sinful person who violated God's commandments and avoided personal responsibility for your disrespectable behavior. Up until 1970 there was no such thing as "no-fault" divorce. Instead, you had to prove your partner was guilty of personal wrongdoing (usually adultery or physical abuse). Women were indeed considered second-class citizens in the social and economic arenas. As writer Lindsay Van Gelder recalls, "Much of the world found feminism hilarious. News of the first big women's march in 1970 . . . was introduced on WABC-TV with the remark 'And now for another item of trivia . . .' Rape victims in those days were generally assumed to have asked for it. The *New York Times* Help Wanted ads were segregated according to gender. Wearing a pants suit to a Manhattan restaurant was a rebellious act. . ." (*The Nation*, Aug. 11–18, 1997).

In those days a man could support an entire family with his one salary. It was assumed that if his wife worked it meant he couldn't support her; he was considered a failure.

If a woman had young children to support, she automatically was turned down for a job. Pat recalls, "When I applied for jobs at that time I had to take my two young daughters in my car with me. I told them to lie down in the car so no one would see them, like the persons interviewing me for work. I knew that I would lose the job if the interviewer saw them. I had to say I had no children to get work. But I usually was found out when one of my kids became ill and I had to stay home to care for her. That meant the end of the job because I would be fired."

As for men twenty-five years ago, you could expect to be employed on a full-time basis at a decent salary with health, pension, and vacation benefits automatically provided by the company you worked for. You knew that the firm you worked for would be in existence ten or twenty years from now, so planning for the future was possible. The harder you worked the more you got paid, and therefore your children would lead a better life than you did, for that was the American Way.

But when Rip Van Winkle awoke twenty-five years later this is what he found:

Many of the firms he worked at were gone forever in the great mergers of the 1990s. The largest employer in the U.S. now was the temporary employment agency Manpower, Inc.! In order to make a decent living and secure a good education for his children he would probably need to work at two jobs since most companies had eliminated work benefits such as health insurance and pensions. Twenty-seven million workers now worked at temporary jobs that gave them less than forty hours a week of work and did not include overtime pay, nor did they provide vacation pay, let alone health and pension benefits. In fact one-third of all Americans had to work at two or more jobs to make ends meet. The shop you worked in today might leave town for Mexico tomorrow and leave you stranded. The only security a worker could now count on was insecurity. Intensified family stress was now an element of daily life. . . .

And where were the women of yesteryear? The non-complaining housewives who accepted their second-class citizenship fate as "normal" weren't around. Instead, women were now working in the business world and trying to find good child-care facilities while they were on the job. Many of them began college or completed the college careers they abandoned for marriage. Pat recalls that after her divorce she returned to complete her college education, which she had regretted abandoning for marriage. "In fear and trembling I went back to college in my mid-thirties thinking I was too old and that my mind would be rusty," she said. "But that turned out to be false. Instead I discovered many other women my age or older were also taking the courses I was taking and that as a group we were smarter than the young kids in the classes. In part we older students were called DARs—that's for Damned Average Raisers, because we got better grades than the twenty-year-olds!"

While Rip Van Winkle was sleeping, women had created a feminist revolution. No, it wasn't a bloody revolution, but a determined one in which women claimed their own sense of self-esteem and demanded social and economic equality with men. While the fight for that equality still continues, it certainly is well on its way to victory.

Rip Van Winkle would be surprised to discover that becoming forty wasn't being "old" anymore. In 1973, forty meant the beginning of the end of life, preparing for a rocking-chair existence. Becoming old meant becoming useless. But in the subsequent twenty-five years an adult-age revolution (along with the feminist revolution) took place. New scientific findings revealed that by nurturing one's body and mind, being forty, or fifty, or sixty-plus allowed for a vigorous, interesting existence—chances for a second or third career, new hobbies, new education and travel possibilities. And contrary to conventional wisdom, one's mind could grow sharper over ongoing years. It's only when you don't use it, as the saying goes, that you lose it.

Because the baby boomers (one-third of the American population) were now in their middle years, and rock star baby-boom idols like the Beatles and the Rolling Stones were turning fifty, this generation had no intention of becoming old and useless. Older yes, useless no. From the middle years on, there is a second chance for us all. Even the definition of "old" has changed: The fastest growing population is now the eighty-five-plus generation—three million today, six million in 2010! Sixty is now a late middle-years number.

Pat and I established our psychological divorce counseling center in 1975 in response to the enormous need for a center that specialized in helping the divorced, which was nonexistent until then. I had by that time received thousands of letters in response to my *Creative Divorce* book, many of them asking for specific help beyond what any book could give them. In response to that need, our Creative Divorce Love and Marriage Counseling Center in San Rafael, California, was created, and we still practice helping our clients every day in their interpersonal problems—from divorce to living together arrangements to premarital counseling to marriage problems to children to dysfunctional family situations.

In fact, it is from our ongoing counseling of divorced men and women and people contemplating divorce that we learned that the 1990s requires an entirely new book, a new *Creative Divorce* book, that takes into consideration all of the new problems as well as new opportunities divorced persons are facing in today's times. In addition, our social and economic order has changed so astoundingly in the past twenty-five years as to render a new book on divorce essential. We could find no other book amongst the glut of divorce books on the market today meeting the specific needs that our Creative Divorce work fulfills. Consider, for example, these changes in the past twenty-five years:

- No-fault divorce is now available in all states. This permits couples to divorce by mutual consent (known as "bilateral" no-fault divorce). However, in forty states, including California (in which Pat and I live), "unilateral" no-fault divorce is permitted. This allows one partner to divorce, even though the other may want to stay married. There is no blame attached to this procedure. Before 1970, proof that one was guilty of wrongdoing (desertion, assault and battery, adultery, drug abuse) was required if divorce was to occur. This meant bitter adversary battles and expensive legal fees were the norm rather than the exception in divorce cases.

- The impact of the women's movement has transformed the self-image of women today. Instead of believing they had no career except marriage to look forward to in life, they have demonstrated their courage, ability, and will to succeed in all areas of public life. It is neither shameful nor outrageous for women to work at careers of their own choosing, whether or not they have children, and they are doing so as a matter of course. Yet a mere twenty-five years ago this new "normal" fact of life was undreamed of.
- Because of this economic and social independence, more women than men are filing for divorce in these times. Before it was a man's prerogative to initiate a divorce since women had no economic base of their own to fall back on. They had to suffer in silence, a consequence of their profound insecurity. Now they can exercise their own choice to either remain married or to divorce.
- With women refusing to take second place to men, tremendous confusion exists in today's gender relations. There is no longer a single standard for relationships to live by. It was all so simple a few decades ago! Men determined all the major decisions in family life, including when to divorce; they knew they were "top dog" in the dating scene (they called first and paid for everything), expecting in return total deference (and sex) from the women they dated. "How do I prove I'm a man? What do women now want from men that they never wanted

before? Why are men more willing to remarry if divorced than women?" These are some of the major questions men are asking these days, and realistically helpful answers are needed.

- With the advent of the new adult-age revolution in the past two decades, there is now a second chance for happiness for divorced men and women who are in their mid-thirties, forties, fifties, or over. It is never too late: witness the new phenomenon of "Start-Over Dads" (referred to as "SODs") in which divorced men quite late in life (Tony Randall in his mid-seventies, for example) are having children in new marriages, hoping to improve their nurturing abilities, which they neglected in their previous marriages.
- A new Sandwich Generation has emerged. Now that people are living much longer (the average life expectancy today is seventy-seven as compared to forty-nine at the beginning of the twentieth century), men and women in their middle years are "sandwiched" between their own children and their ailing parents. Pat and I have heard of situations where divorced persons in their mid-forties have the obligation to support their own children *and* their ailing parents who might be seventy years old or older. Self-renewal after a divorce becomes difficult indeed under such circumstances.
- The new job insecurity status of America's workforce is causing divorces. Recent mergers and downsizing have changed the nature of job entitlements: permanent job status is now a thing of the

past. Jobs are now being transformed into temporary positions, with a consequent loss of pensions and health insurance benefits. This has created very stressful new problems for American families, who can no longer count on a stable future. This fact is resulting in new causes for divorce because of increased family tensions over uncertain futures.

- The phenomenon of "Nomad Dads" has been created, which is the consequence of the enormous downsizing of middle class management caused by the shift from an industrial society to an information society. "Nomad Dads" are the men who have been forced to commute long distances from where they live because their jobs have been eliminated and they can only find temporary work in distant communities. In our counseling practice, my wife and I see people who live in the San Francisco Bay Area but must commute to such places as Los Angeles or Dallas or Chicago to get work at a decent income. They return to their San Francisco homes on weekends or every other week. This causes terrible disruption in family life and often leads to a divorce that would not have happened if such downsizing and commuting didn't exist.
- In recent years, there has been a significant rise in serial divorces and serial remarriages. More and more men and women are divorcing at least two or three times and remarrying after each divorce. This occurs as a result of repeating the past rather than learning from it.

Attending helpfully and constructively to the above issues is central to this book. We believe that today's times requires *The New Creative Divorce* as urgently as the early seventies needed our first *Creative Divorce* book. There is now a new national attack on divorce as being inherently shameful, disgraceful, and wicked, with legislation prepared in over twenty states trying to eliminate their no-fault divorce laws. The dark days of private investigators proving adultery, bitter adversary battles, and long delays in divorce proceedings threaten to return. A concept called "Covenant Marriage" is being promulgated; it would require a two-year separation or proof of fault like adultery or desertion or physical abuse for a divorce to occur.

Given this threat to the more sensible, nonadversarial ways of dealing with divorce that have been the trend of the last twenty-five years, we believe that a clarion call in defense of divorce (as an opportunity, *not* an inevitability) is needed. The current attacks on divorce as a violation of good family values is a fraudulent, cynical maneuver on the part of power elites designed to deflect attention from the real social and economic causes that create divorce problems. Scapegoating divorce by proclaiming that the married couple, family way of life is the only honorable way society's ailments can be overcome appears to be the order of the day. Ironically, the list of enthusiastic proponents of demeaning the divorced include Bob Dole, Newt Gingrich, and Peggy Noonan—all of whom have been divorced! Pseudo-social science authorities manipulate data and surveys to convey "scientific" proof that family breakdown due to divorce is the cause of almost everything wrong in our society, from poverty to violence to drug addiction to teenage pregnancy to crime in the streets and murder. Divorced men and women are labeled losers and self-centered failures by the conventional wisdom spokespersons. This becomes a form of brainwashing: the divorced victims of this assault then begin to internalize this repetitive conventional wisdom and all too often become convinced that indeed there must be something wrong with them because of the divorce.

We see this end result occurring daily in our divorce practice. We have been counseling divorced men and women and their children at our Creative Divorce Love and Marriage Counseling Center in California for the past twenty-three years and have observed the pernicious effect of social science academicians' and media pundits' gloom-and-doom pronouncements on divorced men and women and their children who come to us for help in trying to better their condition.

How often have we heard a concerned single mother say to us, "Am I really a bad parent? I just heard on a talk show that divorce scars a child for life!" Or a sixteen-year-old child of divorced parents will say, "Sure I smoke pot and cut classes, what do you expect? My parents are divorced and the doctor I heard on the talk show the other day said divorce screws up kids." Or a divorced man will say, "I read that if you're divorced it means your next marriage will fail, too. I'm scared to commit myself to a new relationship."

There is a paramount need to explode this conventional wisdom that is scapegoating divorce, for it is the pervasive national repetition of this conventional wisdom that is causing untold damage to divorced people's lives. Our research over the last twenty years demonstrates that the glamorization of the "intact" family (implying that marriage is the only way to keep a family intact) is based on fantasy rather than fact. Here are some examples of the reality the traditional family values promoters ignore:

- Loveless marriages harm children more than vengeance-free, fair divorces.
- Content is more important than form. A marriage contract guarantees nothing if the marriage is grounded in abuse and submissiveness.
- A supportive social environment will do more to create healthy families (including single-parent households) than scapegoating divorce. This would include stable, well-paying jobs, flex-time, paid leave for family emergencies, health insurance for everyone with all people being able to choose their own doctor, building family-friendly educational and recreational facilities instead of more jails, and a national, quality child-care system, which would employ the unemployed.
- Fathers are not the culprit. The "Deadbeat Dad" label is an outrageous slander that distorts the reality that unemployment and low-paying jobs are the primary causes of nonpayment of child support. Most men dearly love their children and want to support them.
- Economic developments such as corporate downsizing, temporary employment with no benefits,

and an unwillingness to retrain or relocate employees as manufacturers move out of the U.S. and relocate their businesses in foreign countries to take advantage of poverty wages, *not* social or cultural issues, are the causes of many divorce problems.

- A greater guilt burden is imposed on divorced working mothers in the U.S. than in any other industrial country. Support systems such as paid family leave, including leave for pregnancy, and a national child-care and universal health program, which are normal services in other countries, are considered Utopian in the U.S.
- There is a dark as well as a bright side to the way people relate in "intact" families. The family that stays together may stay for the wrong reasons, as noted in this bumper sticker seen on highways: "Unspoken Traditional Family Values: Abuse, Alcoholism, Incest."

We title this book *The New Creative Divorce* because we believe divorced men and women have the right to take charge of their own divorce rather than their divorce taking charge of them, as biased data would have it. We know from the thousands of men and women we have successfully counseled that this is the kind of help they are eagerly seeking: a book that empowers them to take personal responsibility to create a healthy life for themselves out of the traumas of divorce. "Creative" in our title is an action word that means making something new and positive out of your divorce.

As we have noted above, we are living in an unprecedented, revolutionary period in American history, moving from an industrial society to a communication-information society. Since the changes in our society are so vast, rapid, and complex, old ways of coping with divorce problems no longer work. Consequently, modern divorce problems require new approaches if they are to be constructively resolved. *The New Creative Divorce* provides these solutions by being grounded in today's realities.

We have the opportunity in this book to suggest advice from *both* a man's and a woman's point of view. In my first *Creative Divorce* book this was not the case. We believe that this adds insight that ordinarily would be lacking if it had been a man's perspective alone.

Both Pat and I have experienced marriage and divorce personally. We do not believe that divorce is "better" than marriage any more than marriage is "better" than divorce. Divorce and marriage are structures, not solutions. They can be useful structures or harmful ones, depending on how you use them. We ourselves have now been married to each other for two decades. We have tried to use the structure of marriage to improve our lives as separate individuals as well as a couple. We also utilized our separate divorces as attempts to better rather than worsen our lives. Every reader of this book has the same opportunity to have a choice rather than an inevitability. The very fact that you have chosen to read our book indicates you already have chosen hope over despair.

We hope you will find the help you need at the time you need it most from the subsequent chapters in this book. We'll begin in the next chapter with the twenty-one most commonly asked questions about divorce and our answers.

# 1

# THE TWENTY-ONE QUESTIONS MOST OFTEN ASKED ABOUT DIVORCE

When people come to see Pat and me to discuss the possibility of getting divorced, they carry a barrage of questions with them. We thought it best to begin our book with the twenty-one most commonly asked questions about divorce that we have heard from our clients. They are questions dealing with an unknown future. What will a divorced person be facing? It is a future in a new, uncertain world.

As counselors we can help chart that future by answering these questions in a way that offers promise and the possibility of positive change in one's divorce rather than disaster. Since you are reading this book, you may have a personal interest in the answers we present to many of these twenty-one questions. We hope our answers will provide you with solid ground to stand on rather than feeling you are headed toward a country laced with minefields.

# 1.

## What process should a man or woman go through to determine whether or not divorce is in fact the right step to take?

Divorce is never something to be undertaken lightly. Next to the death of a loved one, divorce is the most traumatic event in one's life. Consequently, counseling to see if differences can be reconciled so two people can have a new marriage *within* their marriage rather than a divorce should first be considered before making a final decision. Pat and I have dealt with this possibility in great detail in our book *The Seven Marriages of Your Marriage*.

Love is a forgiveness word, so if there is no love left in the marriage, the possibility of positive change in a couple's relationship is nonexistent and divorce proceedings may be the next step.

Love also means that two people can acknowledge that out of unawareness they have done hurtful things to each other, that they have acted unskillfully and now wish to act skillfully toward each other. A reconciliation rather than a divorce is possible if they both agree to work with a counselor who can help them change their own behavior and the behavior toward each other. This can only happen if there is enough love left in their relationship.

## 2.
## Should a couple stay together for the sake of the children?

There is the story of the old couple who came to a lawyer for a divorce after sixty years of marriage. The lawyer was very surprised. Here they were in their eighties wanting a divorce; so why divorce now? They answered: "We never liked each other all the time we lived together, but we stayed together for the sake of our children and waited until they passed away."

Many parents may indeed stay together because they believe divorce will harm their children. What they fail to realize is that children will pick up the fact that Mom and Dad are chronically unhappy with each other as demonstrated by unresolved shouting arguments, physical violence, alcohol, or drug abuse, and more harm will result from "staying together" than divorcing. In divorce they can have the opportunity of renewing their lives separately and ending their negative behaviors. They also can establish new and better relations with their children, recognizing that adults divorce each other, but one never divorces one's children.

## 3.
## What is the basic problem that causes divorce?

People who want a divorce usually focus on one or two issues, often a poor sexual relationship, squabbles over money, adultery, failure to communicate, violence, alcoholism, or drug addiction. However, these are tip-of-the-iceberg excuses for divorce, because if there is any love left in a relationship, two people can change for the better within the relationship by going to counselors or AA or groups that deal with violence. However, divorce becomes "inevitable" when people begin to think of marriage as an extension of their own personal needs, where you don't see your partner as an individual in his or her own right but solely as your permanent entertainment and service industry. It's built in disaster when you expect your partner to make you happy, for you can only make yourself happy. In a good relationship both you and your partner can enhance your own and each other's happiness, but you cannot create happiness in a partner who feels depressed and resentful and has a low sense of self-esteem.

## 4.
## How can divorce be a positive, creative experience since it involves so much pain and uncertainty?

Since divorce is a major crisis in one's life, it can offer either an opportunity to improve the quality of one's life or it can become a disaster. The old Chinese definition of "crisis" as a time of hopelessness *or* an opportunity for positive change in one's position in life is a choice that can be applied to divorce, for divorce is what you make it. You either believe you are a victim and are damaged goods, or you believe you are capable of making positive things happen in your life as a single person. There are great reserves of personal power and courage which can be tapped in most divorced men and women, and the subsequent chapters of this book paint the way this power can be actualized into making divorce a creative experience. The word "creative" means making something new out of one's situation. It means responding to divorce as a challenge to live a better life instead of continuing to live as if one were the victim of a car crash. Learning from the past instead of repeating it is the key to a brighter tomorrow.

## 5.
## Can there be such a thing as a civilized, friendly divorce, where two people part with no hard feelings and do so calmly, rationally, and reasonably?

That's an illusion. Attempts have been made to ritualize divorce separations, and card manufacturers create "divorce announcements" similar to marriage announcements. However, hurt and trauma are intrinsic to divorce. Since a good marriage is one of the most valuable experiences in life, it is indeed inevitable that feelings of profound pain and disappointment will occur when divorce happens. People don't marry with the intention of getting divorced; they marry out of love and in the hope it will be for life. So that when that hope is shattered, profound emotional disarray is its consequence. There is a mourning process that needs to take place, from anger and despair to a sense of self-renewal, which we will outline in a subsequent chapter. The beginning of a "creative divorce" is to divest oneself of the belief that one "should" be cool, calm, and collected at the point of separation and that there must be something wrong if one's emotions are wildly conflicted. Mixed feelings are the norm, not the exception, and need to be understood instead of denied. In the long run a divorced couple can mellow and become friendlier, but in the short run don't be surprised if these qualities are nonexistent.

## 6.
## How shall I tell my children we are getting divorced?

First, set aside the hurt and anger you might be feeling toward your ex-spouse when you are talking to your children. You and your ex-spouse should remember that your children love you *both*, even though you may dislike each other intensely. Consequently, both parents should set aside their grievances with each other when they talk to the children about the forthcoming divorce. They should do so, if possible, jointly and not go into complicated details. It is best to tell the children that Mom and Dad will be living in separate households, that we are going to get a divorce, but that it has nothing to do with you children; you did not cause this in any way. Both of us love you and will never stop loving you. Adults divorce each other, but they never divorce their children. The only difference will be that Mom and Dad will now be living in separate houses but will always be seeing you, and you will be spending time in both of our households. Wait for your children to ask any further questions rather than your going into extended explanations which would only confuse them. Make your presentation in such a way that you can assure your children that they can count on stable, continued support from both of you.

# 7.
## Won't all my divorce problems end once I get that legal piece of paper that says I'm divorced?

The divorce decree can set the rules for moving forward in your life now that the economic and child custody issues have been tentatively resolved. It can, therefore, give you the courage to begin to live in the present rather than to repeatedly replay the old hurts and grievances of the marriage.

However, a host of new, unanticipated problems can—and usually do—arise after you receive the divorce decree, such as: Why are many of my friends avoiding me? What will my own parents think of me? What if my children don't want to see me even though I have visiting rights? Why is my ex-spouse taking me to court to get more money than she/he received in our divorce settlement? Should I date again? The list of new problems are endless, but you can begin to effectively cope with them once you stop being surprised that your divorce doesn't automatically solve your problems or prevent new problems from arising. Divorce is not a legal piece of paper, it is a process over time that involves letting go of the past and living, instead, in the present.

## 8.

## As a newly divorced woman with two young school-age children, how can I survive? I've been a full-time mother without business skills, I've never lived alone before, and I'm scared.

First of all, become aware that there are a lot of support systems that are available to you (which were not present when Pat and I experienced divorce). You can break out of your fear and isolation. There are women's organizations like the National Organization for Women that can put you in touch with retraining programs. There are nonprofit organizations, such as a Family Service Agency available in most major cities throughout the country, that have divorce support groups and counseling at minimum cost. There are Parents Without Partners groups available that offer assistance to children and where you will find you are not alone since all of the members are struggling with problems like yours. You can attend continuing education classes at your local community college and meet new friends as you focus on a career. Inexpensive resources are at your disposal once you seek them out.

When you see yourself as a person who can make positive things happen instead of believing you are a helpless victim because of your divorce, your fears will diminish and your confidence expand.

## 9.

### My legal divorce ended a month ago, and my friends want me to date again. They want to "fix me up"–should I start to date?

Your friends really want to help you—that's what friends are for. But sometimes helping is not helpful. So if you do not feel like dating, respect your own feelings and tell your friends thanks for their concern about you, but you simply are not ready yet to begin dating. It is taking you time to heal and other priorities, like getting a job, are more important than dating. Respect your own feelings and readiness to move in new directions. Acknowledge the advice of your well-meaning friends, but don't be beholden to that advice if you don't agree with it.

## 10.
## How can I ever trust a person of the opposite sex again?

First, you need to learn to trust yourself to be able to make good decisions. Your experience in your marriage can be your greatest teacher. You know that you only saw the tip of the iceberg in your spouse prior to your marriage. For example, the man you married may have hated his mother and then transferred his dislike to you, he may have been more than just a social drinker, or he may have been the quiet type because he had nothing of interest to say rather than because he was strong.

Or the woman you married may have seemed so nurturing when you were dating but was cold and self-centered after marriage. She may have come from an alcoholic family and was impulsive and dysfunctional in your marriage as a result. . . .

These are some of the clues to look for when you are dating a person seriously. You can trust a person when you focus on his or her actual behavior and learn as much about the family background of that person. The more you learn to become self-reliant in all phases of your new life as a divorced person, the more you will be able to see the person you are dating as a real person instead of as an illusion.

# 11.
## What kind of lawyer should I look for?

Look for a lawyer who wishes to help you *and* your soon-to-be ex-spouse agree to a fair settlement of all the issues in dispute. He/she should encourage you and your ex-to-be to settle as many of the issues as you possibly can without legal intervention.

Always remember that the lawyer you hire is accountable to you. You are the person to say to him/her that you want to minimize legal costs and get a fair settlement without delays. Beware of the lawyer, male or female, who brags about being a "barracuda," a lawyer who will help you "get even" with your spouse and exact the last pound of flesh in the process of doing so. That lawyer will get *your* pound of flesh instead. For he/she will raise your legal bills by dragging out your case endlessly with antagonistic briefs and extended court appearances. He/she will be laughing all the way to the bank with *your* money. For no lawyer can help you "get even" with your spouse. All a lawyer can do is assist you to end the legal aspects of the divorce quickly and fairly. These legal aspects are *not* the hurt, pain, anger, or dismay you may feel. Your lawyer is not your therapist but is there to help you sort out the economics of your situation, not your hurt feelings. In fact, a good lawyer will recommend that you seek a divorce psychologist should your feelings distort your ability to see your legal problems clearly.

Don't hire a lawyer blindly. Check around among your divorced friends and acquaintances who have had good experiences with their lawyers. Interview these lawyers and hire the one who is not interested in destroying your former partner but in resolving issues fairly in a way that can help you move your life ahead, rather than replay the regrets and anger of the past.

## 12.
## Is there happiness without marriage?

Yes, but only if you create your own happiness. You are the person in charge of your happiness—and also your unhappiness. You cannot expect someone else to make you happy if you yourself are sad about your situation in life. As a newly single person you are now accountable to no one but yourself to explore new possibilities that can generate interest, excitement, zest, and passion in your life.

You are now living in a far more tolerant society than existed a few decades ago. As a new single woman you will not be labeled unfortunate or eccentric because you are not married. In today's times you are respected for who you are, not whether or not there is a wedding ring on your finger. Similarly men need not feel apologetic for being divorced (after all, one out of two marriages in our society end in divorce so you are one among similar millions!). You will only think of yourself as a "failed person" if you see yourself as such. A change in your attitude so that you reach out to explore new hobbies, a new career, making new friends, joining new groups, and taking advantage of new travel opportunities can add the zest in your life you wish for.

## 13.
## Will divorce scar my children for life?

The answer is no, it will not—but only if you and your ex-spouse prevent it from happening. How you and your ex-spouse handle your divorce will determine whether or not your children will suffer long-term problems out of the divorce. You and your ex-spouse are the first and most important role models for your children. Consequently if you act like a helpless victim, blaming everything on your divorce, your children will believe they also are victims and will use the divorce as an excuse to cut school, avoid studying, involve themselves in anti-social activities such as smoking, using drugs and alcohol, or engaging in dangerous sexual activity.

Your children will indeed be scarred if you and your ex-spouse use them as spies on your former partner's behavior. And should you use your children as weapons to "get even" with your ex-spouse by refusing visitation rights, you are bound to create hostility in your children. You will indeed scar their self-image if you bad-mouth your ex-spouse in their presence and demand they take your side in continuing battles. Your children derive one-half of themselves from you and the other half from your ex-spouse, so when you defame your ex-spouse, you are in effect telling your children that one-half of themselves is bad. Feelings of worthlessness are then generated in your children.

You can eliminate these dangers to your children's long-term welfare by making positive things happen in your life now that you're single again. Instead of seeing yourself as a victim and whining over how sad your fate is because of your divorce, you can demonstrate to your children that, yes, divorce hurts, but that it was necessary, and that your love and caring for your children will last a lifetime. You show that love and caring by not bad-mouthing your ex-spouse, nor limiting visitation rights. If you are the non-custodial parent, you always will remain in touch with your children, *never* considering yourself an outsider. You will also try to influence your ex-spouse to act in the best interest of your children even if you continue to dislike each other.

When you demonstrate to your children that the difficulties in your divorce are challenges to be overcome rather than disasters, you will be giving your children one of the most important positive lessons in their lives: You are showing them that divorce is one of *many* difficulties they may have to face later on in life, such as illness, unemployment, a breakup of a love affair, or a serious accident. You demonstrate to them by how you handle these difficulties that you can prevail over them by acting skillfully instead of becoming victimized by them.

In recent times we have been overwhelmed by the media and self-styled "divorce experts" stating that divorce inevitably traumatizes children for life. Eliminate this false nonsense from your mind. Many elements in life other than divorce can traumatize a person—but only if you allow that to happen. Always remember your children are very resilient. They can bounce back from adversity when you act toward them in a loving way that builds up their self-esteem.

## 14.

### Isn't finding the right person to marry a matter of luck? I was unlucky the last time, that's why I'm divorced. Maybe I'll be luckier the next time.

This attitude will ensure your being unlucky the next time! For it's the product of being brainwashed by seeing too many movies and TV sitcoms in which luck is the answer to all relationship problems. Knowing yourself and the person you believe you may marry the second time around is of paramount importance. Your backgrounds, your value systems, your lifestyles, your empathic connection, your hobbies and interests, your communication abilities—all of these factors need to be carefully considered before a final judgment as to your compatibility with each other can be made. The chemistry between the two of you is not sufficient in and of itself to create a good, lasting relationship. Of course good chemistry is necessary, but beware of falling in lust rather than in love, since love involves compatibility in the other factors noted above.

Luck may give you the opportunity to meet a compatible person. But it is no substitute for working together with that person to make a lasting relationship happen.

## 15.

### How can I make my own mother and father understand my divorce? Will they think I'm a failure and a bad person for getting divorced?

Don't try to postpone telling your parents about your divorce because you are afraid they might disapprove of you. Your parents, if they are typical, are much wiser and observant than you may give them credit for being. Many of our divorced clients have told us how surprised, relieved, and happy they were to find their parents were fully supportive of their decisions once they told them of the divorce. Parents love their children and want them to be happy, no matter how old the children are. So if you are in your thirties or forties, or even older, you can expect a warm welcome from your parents who will not only validate your decision but wish to help you in every possible way. You may also be surprised (as many of our clients have been!) to find out that your parents long suspected there were grave difficulties in your marriage. They never said anything about that fact because they did not want to interfere in your marriage!

## 16.

### Who gets custody of our friends? We made a lot of friends while we were married. Will they now choose sides and avoid seeing me?

Your friends will have mixed reactions to your divorce. Some of your married friends may want to avoid both you and your ex-spouse because they themselves feel threatened by your divorce if their own marriage is sour. They may be shocked because they believed you had a better marriage than they did. (Pat said many of her own friends told her long after her divorce that they indeed were shocked because they thought she and her husband had the best marriage in their neighborhood, so that what happened to Pat might happen to them!) Such friends, afraid to divorce from their own unhappy marriages, may avoid you because you have done what they may want to do but are fearful of doing. Don't be surprised if this happens to you; understand it is their problem, not yours, that they are experiencing.

Some friends may call you up and take your side, while others may do so with your ex-spouse. This also is normal. On the other hand, many friends may still want to continue their friendship with both of you but are at a loss to know how to do so. You may think they should call you up, but they usually will not because they don't know how you will react. It is up to you, therefore, to initiate contact with them. Call them up and you may be happily surprised to find out how much they still care about you.

There is also another category of friends you may discover were simply acquaintances with whom you shared baby-sitting arrangements and went shopping. Once you no longer have these activities in common, your relationship may end. Don't consider this a rejection of you, it is simply that they were less than real friends in the first place and found you useful only for the activities you were mutually engaged in.

In the long run you will find the need to make *new* friends on your own as a newly single person as well as keeping the true friends from your past.

## 17.
## Shall I tell the people where I work that I am getting a divorce?

There is no need to hide your pain. Your coworkers will sense that you are going through some hurtful experience, so you will be fooling yourself if you think you are hiding your dismay. Coworkers usually sense something is wrong and may fantasize dire things about you if you do not tell them what is happening. In these times, it is perfectly appropriate to share the fact that you are going through a divorce. A few decades ago it would be a dirty little secret, because you could be fired if the boss found out you were divorcing. That is not the case today, since you are protected legally from this happening. In addition, you will find, if you're in a typical office, a lot of sympathy from your coworkers, since many of them have themselves experienced divorce. In fact, they can be helpful to you by sharing their experiences on how to skillfully deal with some of the same problems you are facing.

## 18.
## I have been friendly with my ex-spouse's parents and our children love them. Must I, as a mother, deprive my children of seeing their grandparents? And should I personally avoid seeing them, since my ex-spouse and I are on very bad terms with each other? Will his parents take his side and reject me?

Just like your own parents, the parents of your ex-spouse usually are far more objective than you may give them credit for being. So reach out to them—by writing or calling or visiting—and explain how you still want to be friendly with them and to have their grandchildren visit them. These parents of your ex-spouse may tell you—just like your own parents!—that they observed the unhappiness in your marriage but did not want to involve themselves in your personal affairs. They may say how much they love their grandchildren and welcome remaining friends with you regardless of your feelings about their son and vice versa. In Pat's and my experience this is by far the most common result our clients tell us about. So take the risk of contacting them!

## 19.
### I'm a mother with young children. Will I have to lose the house that I love now that I'm divorcing?

No, you don't have to lose your house. A house is part of the economic settlement in a divorce and usually women with children negotiate with their ex-spouse as to how long they will stay. If the ex-husband acts in the best interest of his children, he will either agree to give the house to his ex-wife in exchange for some other aspect of their economic settlement, or he will agree that the house should be sold in a given number of years (often three to five years or when the children reach adulthood) and the profits divided between them.

When an ex-husband is vengeful or vindictive and wants to "get even" with his former wife, he will frequently demand to sell their house immediately so he can get the cash settlement as soon as possible. Of course, this can hurt his children, who may benefit from the stability of remaining in their local school and neighborhood and near their good friends. The courts usually intervene in such cases and try to prevent an immediate sale from happening. A good lawyer, in this instance, can gain for you the protection against such a sale.

In a bitter divorce couples know very well how to hurt each other. For most women, a major pocket of vulnerability is their fear of losing their house. Women view a house primarily as a nesting place, while men see it as an investment that can be converted into cash. So what better way for a vindictive former husband to "get even" with an ex-wife than to demand she immediately vacate the house she loves.

As a man, avoid this trap, which can only generate lasting hostility, which will damage yourself and your children. Settle for a reasonable time limit. Often women will agree to sell their house in five years. But, paradoxically, as a couple heals and overcomes the initial pain of the divorce, an ex-wife will usually initiate selling the house long before the five-year limit. She will find it too big for her new needs as a divorced person and no will longer need the "cocoon" of her old house to nurture her. She has learned instead to nurture herself.

# 20.
## How can a divorce counselor help me?

An experienced divorce counselor will enable you to understand and take charge of the conflicting emotions that a recently divorced person usually experiences. He or she will help you lay the past to rest at the emotional level.

Your lawyers, on the other hand, can only help you at the economic level and give you the groundwork to take charge of your economic life as a single person. Too many divorced persons expect their lawyers to give them emotional support and are disappointed when they find their lawyers cannot do so. Avoid the lawyer who acts like a psychologist; he/she usually has neither the training nor the ability to be helpful in this arena.

A good divorce counselor gives specific help to you at the time you need that help the most. Pat and I counsel as a man/woman team, so if you came to us as an individual seeking a divorce, going through one, or living a post-divorce life in disarray, you would get the sensitivity of what to expect from a couple who know how *both* women and men can respond to the divorce experience.

If you need specific help, we do not hesitate to suggest ways in which, for example, to find a good lawyer and what that lawyer can and cannot do for you. We help you to understand that divorce is a long-term process and not just a legal piece of paper. Along with your economic divorce we help you understand that you are living through an emotional divorce as well. The nature of that divorce consists of riding a roller coaster of conflicting emotions, such as anger, regret, betrayal, love-and-hate, vulnerability, victimization, vengefulness. We educate you to understand that *all* of your feelings are neither good nor bad but are simply present within you to be understood rather than labeled negatively. We help you avoid the blame-making trap and concentrate on acting skillfully so you can live in the present rather than repeatedly replaying the past. We focus on living well as the best form of revenge. To do so means letting go of vengeance, for vengeance hurts no one more than yourself, or your children if you have them.

A good divorce counselor will help you with the parenting skills you might need in your divorce situation (Pat and I have two daughters each). You should expect a divorce counselor to help you find new resources like good career training, and new places where you can meet interesting people should you wish to do so.

Above all, a good divorce counselor can reassure you that you are perfectly normal if you have wild swings of emotion and very mixed feelings as you are going through your divorce. Every divorced person initially feels he or she is the *only* person to ever experience the anguish he or she is experiencing. Certainly Pat and I felt that way in the initial stages of our own divorces. It is enormously reassuring to discover through a good divorce counselor that what you are experiencing is perfectly normal, and has also been experienced by millions of other divorced men and women.

When you understand you are not alone, your healing process begins.

## 21.
## I'm thinking of marrying, but I've been told by some of my friends that I ought to get a prenuptial agreement in case I get divorced later on. Won't that take the love out of my marriage?

No, it will not. In fact it can be a reminder that your marriage has to be worked at and renewed each day, so that you never will be divorced! Only a few decades ago, when Pat and I were both divorced, a prenuptial agreement was unthinkable since it was presumed that only the very rich and famous engaged in such an agreement. And it also was presumed that it indeed would take the love out of a marriage and make your relationship a cold cash arrangement instead.

However, in today's times it is part of the culture of divorce for average couples to agree to a prenuptial agreement if they have separate investments or inheritance rights at the time they decide to marry. Instead of focusing on economics in place of love, a prenuptial agreement can clear the air and eliminate potential bitter hassles that might occur in the future if a divorce should occur. Nobody can predict the future. The reality in the present is that two people love each other and wish to marry for life. But, as John Lennon once said, "Life is what happens to us while we are making other plans." So attention should be paid to prenuptial considerations.

However, no agreement should ever be entered into in advance of a marriage if one partner insists on his or her demands and arrangements to the exclusion of the other partner's needs. There should be an agreement that is fair, which means it is based on two equal individuals deciding and agreeing together on what should appropriately be incorporated into such an agreement. A prenuptial agreement that is based on intimidation (as in a demand like "If you don't sign, I won't marry you") is a sure guarantee that the future marriage is doomed in advance. For a marriage based on a power relationship is a divorce in the making.

A prenuptial agreement is a personal choice two equal people make. Since it is a choice, you can either agree to such an arrangement, or believe it will inhibit the love you have for each other. Pat and I believe this free choice is absolutely necessary if you are to start happily in a marriage. In today's times you are free to do what you wish. However, it is essential that you and your partner be fully aware in advance as to the plusses and minuses of a prenuptial agreement before making a final decision, which may involve contacting a mutually agreed-upon, responsible lawyer.

• • •

As you can see from reading these twenty-one questions and answers, divorce is not simply a legal piece of paper. Instead, it is a journey through new situations. Your courage and willingness to confront the new situations that will arise in your life as challenges to prevail over rather than as afflictions to sink under is what we wish to validate in this book.

Our subsequent chapters are the road map of divorce that thousands of our clients have utilized to make their divorce a truly creative experience. They discovered that the unknown ceases to have any power over them once it becomes known and understood. We invite you to take their journey also, which begins on the next page.

# 2

# A CREATIVE DIVORCE BEGINS WITH SELF-EMPOWERMENT

We have said that divorce is a process over time, not simply a legal piece of paper, and that the divorce process continues long after that legal piece of paper that says "divorce granted" is in your hands.

You can make of this process a journey of self-discovery in which you can learn from your past life rather than repeat it, so that your new horizon becomes bright with possibility rather than bleak with hopelessness. As a newly divorced person you have a choice rather than an inevitability: you have the freedom to choose to see yourself as a person who can make positive new things happen in your life, or as a person who is a victim of life's unfairness.

If you are at the very earliest stage in your divorce, this might seem like a strange statement to make. "What freedom do I have?" you may be saying. "It's taking all of my effort just to be able to survive each day. As a result of my divorce I'm economically strapped and constantly worried about how I can provide for myself and my kids. I feel torn apart inside about my feelings toward my ex-spouse. Sometimes I hate him/her with a passion, other times I feel maybe we could have made it, but then I realize that's a fantasy. I'm confused, hurt, sad, angry, and above all scared over what the future holds for me."

In the initial stage of divorce it seems as if fear is controlling you. I can remember my own fear during that time when I felt severed from my previous home and scared about my future. And Pat remembers how she spent hours crying and feeling sorry for herself, worrying if she could survive the next day and take care of her two daughters who were in their early teens.

How then do we maintain our courage and believe that there is *real* light at the end of our very dark tunnel, not the light of an oncoming train?

- *First become aware that you are not alone.* Millions of other divorced men and women have experienced feelings similar to yours and have subsequently survived as single individuals very well. It only *seems* as if no one else has experienced your pain and uncertainty, because they are your feelings. You can derive reassurance that you are not "helpless" or "going crazy" by understanding that you have joined the ranks of millions of others (in fact, over two million men and women get divorced each year and one million children are involved!) whose range of roller coaster emotions were similar to yours.

- *Recognizing you are not alone enables you to identify your feelings and begin the grieving process of divorce.* Letting go of the past allows you to make way for your self-renewal in the present. The tears, regrets, sadness, anger, bitterness, rage, sorrow, and fears are expressions of the mourning process of divorce, which acknowledges the reality that your marriage is now becoming a part of your past rather than your present.
- *Acknowledge the nobility in the initial mourning stage over the loss of your marriage.* To experience the end of your marriage as a death—the death of a relationship—is to acknowledge its profound meaningfulness. As we have remarked, next to the actual death of a loved one, divorce, being the death of a relationship, is the second most traumatic experience in life. Consequently, you are validating the humanity within you when you are grieving over what is indeed a profound loss in your life. No matter what you may be feeling about your ex-spouse now, you married initially out of the best intentions, out of feelings of love and the desire to share your life with your partner in order to enhance the happiness of both of you. What could be more valuable? It would be strange indeed if you didn't feel intensely the loss of the life you hoped for.
- *You can shore up your courage when you acknowledge to yourself that nothing lasts forever.* That means that your current feelings also are not forever, it only seems like they are at the time you are experiencing

them. I can recall how I felt I couldn't survive on my own during the first month of my divorce, but six months later I could only marvel that I ever felt that way. And Pat felt she could never trust another man again or marry one, yet five years after her divorce we two married each other. I remember being quoted in my local newspaper a year after my divorce as saying I could never marry again (I, too, felt the opposite sex untrustworthy). Yet five years after my divorce that feeling of fear of the opposite sex was part of a forgotten past. The bleak hopelessness you may be feeling now may turn into bright hope months from now once you see new possibilities ahead of you.

- *Draw upon your memory bank of survival techniques from your own past.* Your divorce is not the first crisis in your life. Think back to the times in the past when you thought you couldn't survive, and yet you survived very well. The first time you left home for school? Applying for and holding down your first job? The lover that rejected you? The illness that was life-threatening? A death in the family? Losing a job? Supporting a family and raising children? All of these challenges in life—and many more—you may have prevailed over before your divorce. So you're not the helpless victim you may try to convince yourself you are. You have a track record of making positive things happen in your life. Divorce is another challenge to you to make positive things happen once again.

- *Stop seeing yourself as a victim.* When you act toward your ex-spouse out of vengeance and blame him/her for all the "bad" things in your now-single life, you are shooting yourself in the foot. You are acting out the role of a helpless person who fears taking personal responsibility to move one's life ahead and instead keeps fighting the battles of the past.

  You begin to end your self-victimization when you recognize that you and your ex-spouse are not now and never were villains acting maliciously to undermine each other. Instead, you were two decent people who loved each other at the time of your marriage and through unawareness did hurtful and harmful things to each other. Not knowing how to act skillfully to resolve these difficulties resulted in the erosion of your relationship. Instead of blaming each other, which is a victim's way of acting, you can begin to take positive charge of your new life as a single person by acknowledging this truth. Become aware that you acted unskillfully and now in your single state prepare to seek out the ways to act skillfully, not to redo the past but to improve your life in the present.

  Divorce is the time to put into practice that marvelous Chinese saying: "It is better to light one candle than to curse the darkness a thousand times."

- There is the story of the man who went to the paint store, bought some yellow-orange paint, and then painted five horizontal stripes of that color on one of his living room walls. He stared at what he had done and then yelled out in panic, "Help! Help! There's a tiger in my room!"

In other words, you may be scaring yourself half to death by obsessing over the fearful consequences of your divorce, without realizing that much of that fear is self-created. You are stronger than you may think you are. For example, we see many divorced women who say they would like to return to school and seek a career but fear they have no ability to pass the courses involved. We frequently get a call or a warm letter from such women a few years later stating proudly that they indeed returned to school and obtained their degree!

• • •

## Mourning Your Divorce: The Healing Process at Work

As we noted, mourning the emotional death of your relationship, which is your divorce, is as natural and normal as mourning the physical death of a loved one. And just as mourning the physical death of a loved one is the way of returning to health and self-renewal, so too is mourning your divorce the way to the same goals.

Don't be surprised should your mourning process begin *after* you are served the legal papers notifying that the divorce is final. For it is the *emotional* divorce that you are experiencing in the mourning process. This timing is what most divorced men and women experience. If the rush of contradictory feelings you may be experiencing shocks you because you never expected these feelings to occur (after all, weren't you fantasizing how wonderful your life would be once you were rid of that "turkey" partner of yours?), your very health requires you to accept these feelings as a normal consequence of your divorce. If you deny those feelings or are ashamed or embarrassed because you can't control them (and therefore put on a false face of pretended happiness to people at large in order to mask your fears of your emotional overload), you will internalize your grief and suffer the consequences of possible depression or physical illness.

Mourning the death of a marriage is more than just a one-time outburst of anguished feelings, it is, instead, a time-healing process that can enable you to become a person who takes charge of his or her life positively rather than one who sees life as a series of disasters waiting to happen. To accomplish this goal, divorced men and women typically move through four stages that are inherent in the mourning process.

### 1. The "Why Me?" Stage

There is initially the shock of the unexpected. The separation you once hoped for becomes a nightmare of negative surprises: you can't sleep or eat, you have outbursts of crying for "no reason at all," rage and anger over why this situation has happened to you, survival fears of not being able to make it on your own, denial ("It can't really be true, this is just a nightmare"), bitterness over being singled out for punishment by an unjust God ("I'm a good person, I don't deserve what's happening to me").

## 2. The "If Only" Stage

After the initial shock wears off, you begin to move from denial of the reality of being single to very reluctant acceptance of the need to make it on your own. This becomes the time of sadness and regret over imagined lost opportunities in your marriage, resulting in "If only" flagellations against oneself and one's former partner, such as: If only I wasn't so short-tempered . . . If only my spouse was better in bed . . . If only my spouse wasn't so critical of everything I did . . . If only I had stopped drinking so much . . . If only I had prepared myself for a better job . . . .

Drowning in "If only" becomes the road to despair, which can lead to depression. It convinces you that the present is simply the consequence of missed opportunities in the past and that you are doomed to suffer from guilty regret for the rest of your life. Despair and hopelessness become the defining elements in this stage of the mourning process.

## 3. The "Letting Go" Stage

Paradoxically, hope begins to emerge out of the hopelessness experienced in Stage 2. Feelings of deadness, detachment from people and no desire to make new friends, a general lack of interest in the world around you—these are the feelings and behavior that now take center stage in your life.

Although self-isolation and apathy now prevail, the hopelessness you had been feeling transforms in Stage 3 to the foundation for new hope, since the illusion that you can recapture and remake the past is now swept away. This stage forces you to "detach" yourself from that illusion and provides the grounding for you to move forward in the present rather than remain chained to your past.

### 4. The "Self-Renewal" Stage

The previous three stages pave the way for your self-renewal. The mourning process starts with outrage, pain, and disarray, and a refusal to believe you are single and can survive on your own. The apathy and self-isolation you experience in Stage 3 ends with a recognition that these are signs that you are detaching yourself from your identity as a married person. Gradually, you move toward a recognition that you are indeed divorced and single, and you acknowledge in your emotions that you must now take personal responsibility to make positive things happen on your own.

In the self-renewal stage all of the wide-ranging, anguishing feelings you lived through in the previous three stages have been minimized or purged so that they become memories of your past behavior rather than controlling your present behavior. You empower yourself to live in the present. Self-flagellation turns into self-acceptance.

Knowing that your initial grief has the potential for you to create a better life for yourself in your divorce can be a powerful help to you in acting skillfully rather than angrily and fearfully in your life as a single person. Your awareness of the four stages of the mourning process helps you make sense out of the initial turmoil divorce creates. It encourages you to see hope when things seem hopeless. Mourning tells you, "This too shall pass."

When we explain the mourning process to our clients, they always ask us the following questions.

**How long does the mourning process last?**

Our answer is that there is no specific time limit, for each divorced person grieves in his or her own way. However, it usually lasts within a range of one to two years. For some men and women, the mourning process has already taken place before their legal divorce. They have grieved within their marriage (particularly if that marriage was stressed with physical and emotional abuse, drug or alcohol addiction, or numerous affairs), recognizing that their marriage has already ended. For such people the legal divorce itself becomes a form of liberation rather than an invitation to a scary future.

However, for most other people the mourning process will occur once your separation begins and will end within a range of one to two years. Trust your own feelings when well-intentioned friends tell you to stop being sad and to start dating again, but you feel you are not ready to do so. You can tell your friends you appreciate their concern for you, but you do not feel ready as yet to move in that direction. When you do, you will ask for their help. When you explain this to your friends, you are beginning to practice the self-reliance that is the goal of the completion of the mourning process.

Some newly divorced people believe they must present a stiff upper lip to people in general and deny any need for grieving, even though a cauldron of feelings are boiling inside them. If they continue to deny their feelings and keep pretending everything is fine when everything isn't, they can be stuck in the first stage of the mourning process for a lifetime without ever knowing it; these men and women internalize their bitterness and anger, which can often result in depression and/or physical illnesses such as a stroke or heart attack.

**Does everyone experience the same mourning process?**

Not necessarily. As we noted above, some people have completed the mourning process entirely within a dysfunctional marriage. Others may have gone through the first or second or third stage before their marriage ended and may be ready for their self-renewal in the fourth stage once they have separated.

The feelings erupting in the mourning process are universal—they cut across class lines and racial lines, and appear in citizens of countries throughout the world. Just as your physical self is a self-healing organism when injuries occur, so is your inner self self-healing through the mourning process.

**When will I know my mourning process has ended?**

You will know when your mourning process has ended when you listen to what your feelings are telling you about what you are now ready for in your life. Here are the major feelings that will tell you your mourning process has ended:

- You realize you are not a failure because you are divorced. You recognize that divorce was the only honorable alternative to a marriage that was destroying both you and your spouse (and having a disastrous effect on the children both of you may have).
- You no longer believe your ex-spouse is a monster who made life hell for you but is simply a fallible human being like yourself. So instead of seeking vengeance for all the hurt you experienced, you have stopped obsessing about "getting even." Still feeling a little sad, a little regretful about your past relationship, you begin to focus on how you can better your own life rather than how you can hurt your ex-spouse.
- You become bored with being bored with yourself; the television set becomes a squawking intrusion rather than a comfort; you decide not to drink the next glass of wine or beer. You are then beginning to feel it may be time to break out of your self-isolation.
- You reach out to your friends and surprise them—and yourself!—by calling or e-mailing them for the first time in many months. You needn't feel they will reject you—real friends never do.
- You start to focus on resolving your present problems rather than replaying the past in your mind and feelings for the thousandth time.

- You no longer stereotype all persons of the opposite sex as being "just like my ex-spouse" who must be avoided at all cost because they will hurt you. You began to see people of the opposite sex as individuals and feel that taking someone out might be pleasant rather than a disaster.
- You start to let go of the past when you notice you are spending too much time worrying over the what-might-have-beens in your marriage. You begin to concentrate on living in the present, which means making new friends, seeking out a new hobby, or checking out new career opportunities.
- You begin to see that no one in this world exists to make you happy. You are discovering that you must take personal responsibility for making yourself happy, and that your divorce gives you the opportunity to do so. Whether or not you take advantage of that opportunity is entirely up to you.

• • •

## Self-Empowerment in Spite of Society's Backlash

We have discussed the tendency of newly divorced men and women to view themselves as victims, subject to malign external forces beyond their control, and how the mourning process enables you to overcome this self-imposed view. However, this sense of yourself, to a great degree, is the product of carefully programmed brainwashing by the media and the power elites in our society, who wish to benefit from a population who can be manipulated. What better way to manipulate a population than to create or reinforce the notion that divorced people are failures with weak morals—selfish victims of their own vices.

The propaganda barrage generated by the media and power elites today victimize the divorced population by labeling divorced men and women violators of "traditional family values." As such, we are supposed to be ashamed of our behavior and fade into the woodwork of our society. There was a time, only a few decades ago, when divorce was viewed by the media and power elites as a "sin against God." Now it is being presented as a sin against society and family life committed by irresponsible individuals.

Nothing is more needed for the health of all divorced men and women than to eliminate this nonsense from their thoughts and feelings. The personal pain of divorce is anguishing enough without buying the external pain created by purveyors of the snake oil of alleged "traditional family values." This phrase is revealed as a figment of imagination when it is exposed to the real light of history. The builders of the "traditional family values" myth built it around the 1950s, a decade when divorce was never mentioned, even when it happened, and where lifetime marriages were hailed as the norm no matter how destructive they might be.

What is implied by the peddlers of "traditional family values" is that the 1950s way of life has been "traditional" since the birth of the United States and therefore the only truthful way to live. The changes in family life since the '50s, viewed from this perspective, are all essays in disaster, so a return to this past is believed to be the only positive solution to the family-life problems of today.

However, it is impossible to return to a time that only existed in the imagination. It is an historical fact that family life in the '50s was the *exception* to life as it was lived in previous generations as well as in the generations that have succeeded that time, rather than being the rule. Prior to the '50s, the trend in our society was to marry later in life (in the '50s almost half of all women married in their teens!). And before the '50s, a trend of ever-increasing divorce rates and women working outside the home was "traditional." An historical survey of divorce in the United States was titled *Divorce: An American Tradition* (Oxford University Press, 1990) and demonstrated that divorce was introduced in America by the Puritans in the early 1600s; it pointed out that even in 1956 commentators were labeling the United States "the leading divorce country in the Western world."

Divorce, therefore, is a "traditional" American institution. It is an option, just like marriage, than can be used constructively or destructively. There is nothing "wicked" about divorce any more than what you make of it. If you view it as an opportunity to improve your life, you will eliminate the idea that you are in violation of "traditional family values," since divorce itself is a traditional American value! On the other hand, if you see yourself as a guilt-ridden victim, you will eagerly point to the fiction of "traditional family values" as proof of your unworthiness.

It has been our experience counseling divorced parents and their children over the past two decades that we can only applaud the vast majority of them for their sincere and dedicated efforts to incorporate decent family values into the everyday practice of their lives and into their children's behavior. Can divorced persons with children generate the family values of self-respect, self-esteem, honesty, integrity, decency, empathy, and personal responsibility into their family lives? The answer is forthcoming in the passionate statement of one of our clients, Jody, by name, who wants to tell the divorced men and women who are reading this book about her own experiences as a thirty-eight-year-old divorced person living alone with her three children. She married at nineteen, and when she was thirty-one she divorced her abusive, alcoholic husband. (He had refused to go to counseling with her to see if they could improve their marriage. Instead, he stayed married to alcohol rather than going to Alcoholics Anonymous.)

Here is what she said: "Tell your divorced clients not to give up—don't let anyone intimidate you!" she told us. Her experiences can be replicated by countless other women—and men—who feel the same way: "When I hear people say that single mothers like me don't believe in decent family values and are letting our kids run wild because we are selfish and don't care about them, I get furious. Please excuse the expression, but that's pure bullshit!

"I've always tried to teach my kids the best kind of values like the ones I was taught when I was a little girl, like being honest, taking personal responsibility for my actions, respecting myself and other people, earning what you need instead of demanding a handout. My parents taught me to get as much education as possible, to become a good citizen by helping others and caring about the environment and being kind and unselfish instead of just looking out for number one at the expense of everyone else. These are the values I've taught my children, so when anyone tries to tell me I'm a bad parent, they better watch out. Many of my friends are also single mothers and believe in the same things I do and don't like being told we are irresponsible. We all love our children. Why, the only reason I'm working so hard at two jobs is because I want the best for my three kids. I'm trying to show them that by working so hard I'm taking personal responsibility for their welfare and showing them the value of hard work. After my divorce, I went back to college and completed my degree in marketing and sales and now make good money in software sales. So I show my kids how important education is. I show my love for my kids by providing a roof over their head, good food on their table, decent clothes for them to wear, and educational books and computers for them at home. I'm trying to save money to take them on vacations, and right now I'm trying to buy a home so we'll always have a place to live.

"I would be a moral failure if I just stayed home and looked at TV all day and did nothing with my life, letting my children become vagrants. But that's not true, so don't blame me for what society is doing to our kids. Because no matter how hard I try to raise my kids to become decent, law-abiding citizens, the society we live in today is making matters worse for our children. In order for me to earn a decent living so my children can grow up strong and healthy and secure, I have to work at two jobs. I feel so guilty over not spending enough time with my children. I'm so busy working, so busy trying to stay ahead that I feel my kids are losing out in the long run. That's true not only of myself and my single-mother friends, but also the married couples I know when they both have to work to make ends meet at the expense of spending a little time with their kids.

"Now don't tell me I've failed. It is the system that's failing. The people that run our country should provide programs that would allow more time for people like me to spend with our kids. Like decent child care, which I now can't afford, or flexible hours so that when something happens to my kids I can leave my job to help them without being fired. Or the schools my kids go to—they are run-down and asbestos-ridden. And safety in the streets—I worry every time my kids have to walk home from school, even though it's four blocks away. Only last month one of their friends was almost kidnapped. It's the government that's failing our children, not single mothers like me and my friends. I find it crazy that our government can give Mexico a fifty-billion-dollar handout of our tax money but then says it can find no money for decent health care or child care centers for all the families that need them, better schools and an end to crime in the streets.

"Look at the pollution in our environment and what it is doing to our kids. My youngest daughter suffers from asthma caused by all the smog around; and I worry over our drinking water since it has lead in it. I can't even take my kids on vacation to the favorite river I used to swim in as a kid because it's now loaded with feces, garbage, tin cans and glass fragments. I'm teaching my children the need to protect our environment. We do a lot of recycling, don't smoke, and try to use public transportation as much as possible instead of adding to the smog by always using our car. I worry about the kind of world I'll be leaving my children when I die. We've got to end pollution and stop destroying the rain forests and poisoning animals and fish. And nuclear waste disposal is a terrible nightmare.

"I worry about the food my children eat. No matter how careful I am, I can't protect them against possible bacterial infections that are present in food today, in meat, fruits, and vegetables. It's our government's responsibility to protect our food, yet it is not doing it. I just heard scientific authorities say that bacteria in food causes illnesses in seven million men and women and children each year and nine thousand deaths.

"I see more and more children in my neighborhood starting to smoke, even Joey, a kid of eleven who lives down the block. Yet our government continues to support tobacco farming, and cigarettes are legal. The TV announced the other day that three thousand children each day take up smoking and one thousand of those kids will die from it. So when those same government leaders talk about how they favor family values, does that include favoring killing our children by getting them addicted to cigarettes? The nerve of our leaders to talk about how they are in favor of family values to protect our children while at the same time they are destroying our planet!

"If this country of ours wants us to raise good children, then the companies we work for must pay us decent wages so we won't have to work all the time just to make ends meet. It's the companies that are making us neglect our children when they don't pay enough or give us flexible hours.

"It's a fact that it's not just eligible parents, or married couples, for that matter, that's needed to raise decent kids these days—it's the whole community. You have to be able to rely on your neighbors, the school system, the police department, to work together. For example, if I'm at work and my son is sneaking out of the house that night, my neighbors should be able to take personal responsibility to get in touch with me immediately so I can take action. And the police department needs to back you up when you call for help if your child is in trouble. Most of the time the police are so overwhelmed they do not have the manpower or resources to help teens who are trying to get off drugs. And the schools should be more involved so that when my child cuts school the teacher would notify me immediately instead of telling me two days later that it happened. Because the schools have so little money to spend, they try to get rid of the kids who desperately need help, like those on drugs or who steal, instead of helping them change their ways.

"Instead, the schools label the kids troublemakers and kick them out of school. It makes the problem worse, but it makes it easier on the school. We also need our neighbors to watch when they see some school kids they don't know enter my house while I'm working and possibly steal things for drug money. They should notify me immediately, and I should do the same for them.

"We all feel so powerless, but there is hope. For example, I thought my teenage son, Dennis, who just turned eighteen, was a lost soul when he was in his early teens. He was out of control, I felt, because I wasn't there when he came home from school; I work most of the time and am unable to make dinners or help him with his homework. And he wasn't getting help in his school, since he was stealing, using and dealing drugs, and was a gang member who carried a gun. The school officials were more interested in busting him for using drugs than getting him help. They wanted him arrested.

"You would think Dennis was a lost cause, but he's turned his entire life around now that he's eighteen. Part of the reason why is because I've never given up on him, no matter how far he strayed from the straight and narrow. I set down my values to Dennis and my two girls from day one, and thank God Dennis has gone right back to those values, because they were instilled in him at a very early age, so he never forgot them even when he violated them. Dennis had dropped out of school for two years, but went back and now at eighteen just graduated at the top of his class. He now has a forty-hour-a-week job, and is proud of the fact that he personally earns his own money. His self-esteem is high now because he has earned that esteem. He's not ripping anyone off and is responsible for paying his credit card bill at the end of each month. He's also involved in a teenage recycling club. He's drug free, does not smoke, and uses alcohol only on occasion. He never sees any of his former gang-member friends. He turned his life around because he finally saw that the values I taught him really mattered after all. They hit home to him because he finally realized he was destroying his own life. He saw some of his former gang friends die, while others are now in jail. Half of the girls he knew now have children although they are only fifteen or seventeen years old. He told me he was afraid that his life was going nowhere, too, and was scared. I feel proud that we had a relationship where he felt free to tell me his deepest feelings, because he knew that in spite of our differences I loved him dearly and wanted to help him. He also told me I was right in teaching him the values he had fought against.

"So for anyone who is reading what I'm saying, please, please, have faith that the values you have taught your children in their early years will pay off in the long run, providing you keep the lines of communication open. There will be a time when your children will return to you."

• • •

The passion in Jody's voice as she spoke to us affirmed that she refused to see herself as a victim and made positive things happen in her life in the face of severe problems. It is still a fact that women, married or not, face discrimination in the world of work and only make seventy-five cents for every dollar a man makes in similar jobs. And with downsizing, women are usually the last hired and the first fired so that economic insecurity for people like Jody is further compounded.

Jody, however, has learned to prevail over life's difficulties, rather than drown in self-pity. Just after her interview with us, she said brightly, "I don't want anyone reading what I said to get the impression that I'm a whiner. I criticize things that are not right to make things better. I owe it to my children to make a better life for them."

Then she said with a smile on her face, "Now isn't that a good family value?"

# 3

# DIVORCE CAN TEACH YOU THE TRUE MEANING OF LOVE

It's in the news so often that we take it for granted: the rage and anger and thirst for vengeance of an ex-wife or ex-husband against each other. An ex-husband shoots his ex-wife, his lawyer, or both, and then turns the gun on himself . . . . An ex-wife smashes into her ex-husband's car as she sees him driving away with another woman . . . . An ex-husband burns down the house his ex-wife lives in . . . . An ex-wife falsely accuses her ex-husband of sexually abusing their ten-year-old daughter in order to prevent him from ever seeing her again . . . . And either an ex-wife or ex-husband may wind up in jail for kidnapping their children.

Why? Shouldn't a newly divorced person be happy just "getting rid" of the person he or she now claims to hate? Why not goodbye-and-good-riddance?

The answer can be found in an incident that was prominently reported in newspapers throughout the country: A man in his sixties went to court to get an injunction against his wife because she had been smoking heavily for over forty years. His own mother had died of heart disease from smoking and he didn't want the same thing to happen to his wife. He said he wanted the government "to protect me against having to grow old alone, to protect me against the loss of the love and support and companionship of the woman I love." Indeed she quit smoking as a result of his action. In a very real sense *both* won the case. He did not lose what he considered a part of himself should she die from smoking, and she lengthened her life.

Many married men still use phrases like he did, calling their partner "my better half" or "my good right arm," and in their saying so affirm that this spouse is truly a part of themselves, consciously or unconsciously. That feeling exists in every married couple. So it's not surprising that when a divorce happens many newly divorced women tell us, "I feel as if I'm not a whole person now that I'm no longer a wife." For divorced men and women both, the sense of loss is paramount when they leave each other. A thirty-two-year-old client of ours said that when she told her father she and her husband were "breaking up," he said, "Honey, bricks break, people tear." To "break" means a once-and-for-all ending; to "tear" means to "lacerate," which is to wound, to distress deeply.

It should come as no surprise, therefore, that the tearing apart of divorce generates so much pain, anguish, and hatred. For a psychological tearing away of part of oneself is a severely wounding experience. *Now* you may feel hatred for your ex-spouse, but you married your spouse out of love, and your children, if you have them, are a product of that marital love. Consequently, to hate your partner is to hate a part of yourself, which is why the violence inflicted by a divorced spouse on an ex-partner can turn into suicide as a form of self-punishment.

The very intensity of the feelings people experience in divorce gives the lie to the conventional wisdom that marriage these days is a casually chosen and easily dispensable affair, with saying goodbye as painless as saying hello. Most people marry because they love the person they marry. The love they feel may very well be limited and distorted and self-defeating, but it is love to the best of their understanding at the time they marry. It may take their divorce for them to get the message that love means actively practicing the qualities of empathy, compassion, companionship, friendship, mutual sacrifice, and mature support in an equal relationship. It is such a relationship, in Ford Madox Ford's words, that renews each other's courage and helps cut asunder the inevitable difficulties in life. It is what we call a creative marriage, which can prevent the collision courses that generate a divorce.

To reach this goal, however, requires every individual who experiences divorce to become whole persons instead of feeling as if they are half-persons at the time of their divorce. It is inevitable and appropriate to feel that some things are profoundly lost as a result of your divorce. Most important of all is the loss of love, for the loss of the love-connection creates the feeling of being a half-person at the time one realizes the marriage has ended.

• • •

## A New Look at Love

"What's love got to do with it?" is the cynical title of a popular song.

The answer is *everything!*

Without love nothing matters; that is the reason why divorce has such a devastating impact on anyone involved in a deeply committed, monogamous relationship, whether you call it marriage, a living-together arrangement, or a domestic partnership.

In Pat's and my many divorce group counseling sessions with men and women combined, we find they universally agree that love is the number one necessity in a committed relationship, and that the loss of love in their own past relationship is the black hole inside themselves they are experiencing as the result of their separation.

There is the story of Louis B. Mayer, the powerful head of MGM Movies in the '20s, '30s, and '40s, when it was the outstanding Hollywood studio. He was one of the wealthiest men of his time, who could and did make people jump at the snap of his fingers. He sponsored the successful "family values" movies of that time—the Andy Hardy series, Boystown—but practiced none of the loving-kindness espoused in those films in his own personal life. (His biographers have called him ruthless, paternalistic, and tyrannical.) When he was dying of cancer, an associate asked him in a last hospital visit what words of wisdom he wished to leave to the world. Louis B. Mayer replied,

"Nothing matters." And that included his divorce, which he unfortunately learned nothing from.

Indeed, "Nothing Matters" is the endgame of lives lived without love, an anguished cry of despair.

Becoming a whole person doesn't necessarily mean marrying again, for the choices in our society are many and varied and can lead to satisfying lives without marriage. It can mean, for example, being "married" to a social cause, a church, a person of the same sex, a live-in partnership without a marriage license. But *all* forms of commitment require love as the fundamental glue to piece together a happy and fulfilling life.

Therefore, it is extremely important to understand how and why we love—and what went wrong with the love that was part of your marriage. Learning from the mistakes you've made, and understanding how to avoid repeating them, is a necessary foundation for a creative divorce. Consequently, the balance of this chapter will focus on using your divorce as a learning experience—one that will help you understand the true meaning of love, in place of the mutual self-deceptions practiced by many couples that result in their divorcing.

On the basis of many divorce group counseling sessions we've had, with both men and women present, we'd like to share with you the many ways in which these well-meaning, decent people trapped themselves into believing and practicing forms of love that really weren't authentic. Identifying and understanding these self-deceptions (which we'll call "masquerades") not only will help you understand what went wrong in your marriage, but will help you avoid these self-destructive patterns in the future.

Listed below are the seven predominant types of love masquerades that prevent divorced men and women from giving and receiving the love they want and need.

• • •

## The Seven Self-Deceptions That Masquerade As Love

### 1. The I-Will-Be-Loved-for-What-I-Can-Do-Not-for-Who-I-Am Masquerade

Here is a typical example of a couple's problem that is all too frequently experienced in our society:

Frank and Ellen, married for twelve years, are on the verge of breaking up, but are meeting with us in counseling to see what, if anything, can be salvaged from their relationship. "You don't love me anymore, or maybe you never did," Ellen complains. Frank looks astounded, "How can you say that? Look at the five-bedroom house we have, the Lexus, the swimming pool, the yearly vacations we take to Europe, the great clothes you wear, and the twelve-hour days I put in at the office so our kids could go to the best college. I did it all for you—if that isn't love I don't know what is."

Ellen replied angrily, "You still don't get it—I want you to hug me, to kiss me, to make love to me instead of to the business telephone you're always on. The kids want to know who you are; the only time they ever see you is when you're holed up in the den with the computer or the telephone, making another business call. I want *you*, but there's no "you" there. All you are is a business machine. You're not talking about love when you say you give me things; you're talking about the ego trip you give yourself. Our children never see you so they think you don't love them because you give them presents instead of spending time with them. Don't you understand that tenderness and affection are more important to me than making a buck? I want the old Frank back, the Frank I thought I married. You were so different then."

In this situation Ellen was right. Somewhere along the way Frank had come to believe that his career and bank account were the most important things in his life—that they actually defined who he was. Deep down he thought he had to pay for his family's love. Eventually he began to believe that they should be paying for his "love" too, by serving as appropriate status symbols, and he treated them accordingly.

Ellen shared her experience in her divorce counseling group, because Frank never understood that no person can make another person lovable. Frank had to do this for himself, but he had refused further counseling to eliminate his self-defeating behavior, so Ellen initiated her divorce. "I've since learned," Ellen told her divorce group, "to be more assertive and communicate more directly in my relationships with men. Frank inhibited me, but I now see that I let myself be inhibited, so I really can't blame him for not communicating better."

## 2. The I-Will-Be-Loved-As-a-Man-If-I-Pretend-to-Be-Invulnerable Masquerade

Our society tends to stereotype men, particularly into feeling that they can only be lovable if they are always being in charge of their lives. It is this John Wayne syndrome that is frequently evidenced in our clients who come to our counseling center.

For example, here is Ron and Amy, a couple in their late thirties, married ten years. Ron tells us he can't understand why Amy insisted he come with her to talk about their marriage. But Amy says, "He's been driving me crazy in all of the ten years we've been married. He never tells me what he is feeling. Oh, yes, he'll talk about politics, TV, or the stock market, but whenever I see him look sad or anxious or detached and ask him, he always says, 'It's nothing, I'm fine.' Well, the last straw happened last week. You see, he had been moody and was also looking depressed when he came home from work during the past two months, but he wouldn't say anything. It was like pulling teeth, but I just found out from him that he's been worried because there have been rumors that the company he works for might be merged out of existence, and that he didn't tell me because he said he didn't want to worry me. My God! And for two months I tortured myself every day. I thought he was actually having an affair because we didn't even have sex once during the past two months. He's like a blank page. I'm tired of trying to guess all the time what it is he's really feeling."

She then turned to Ron and said, "My God, do you think I wouldn't love you anymore if you were unemployed?

I would love you if you shared your fears, and, yes, even if you cried about it, and asked for my help."

But Ron was too "proud" to change and their marriage tore apart.

### 3. The Love-Is-a-Possession Masquerade

When a person feels unworthy of being loved, he or she tries to control the other person out of fear that that person would leave the relationship if left to his or her own free will.

For example, Sherry and George, both in their late twenties, have been married three years. Sherry says she is very much in love with George and they have a monogamous relationship. However, she is terribly jealous and has this compulsion to call her husband at his office (he's a lawyer) at least five or six times a day, which makes him angry because it interferes with his work. She says if she doesn't "check up on him" he might be attracted to someone else. She knows this is absurd behavior on her part yet she continues to call him, to the detriment of their relationship. George says he has urged her to see us, since he feels he is being pushed over the edge by her unreasonable jealousy. "Even when I talk to another woman at a party she's furious. I dearly love her but she makes me feel like a little kid who has to account for every minute I'm not with her."

In counseling, we were told by Sherry that her father had always favored her younger sister over herself. She yearned for any crumb of affection he would give her, which hardly ever happened. Consequently, she grew up believing she was unlovable. ("I believed that if I had been as attractive as my sister, Anita, I could have gotten the hugs and kisses I wanted so desperately from Daddy," she told us.) She had transferred the belief that she was unlovable to her relationship with George. "How could he possibly be in love with me—any other woman can easily take him away from me," was what she told us she felt.

She was seeing George as if he were her father (since like her father, he was the most important male figure in her life). She was acting as if she were the frightened, "unlovable" child she felt she once was; she had convinced herself that George would stay with her only if she watched him like a detective every minute of the day. Of course, watching him like that could only end the marriage rather than bring them closer together.

"She continued in her old ways rather than trusting me, so that's why I'm here," George told his divorce group.

### 4. The Love-Means-I-Can't-Survive-on-My-Own Masquerade

When a person is insecure, he or she feels love means never being abandoned by one's partner, even though this can create overreactions that can destroy a relationship. This happens more frequently than might be supposed. A far-from-exceptional example occurred at our counseling center recently:

Kate and David, married ten years, say they can't stand living together. David says she embarrasses him by screaming angrily in front of his staff (he's a sales manager selling recreational property leases). She visits him frequently for lunch at his worksite, where there is always a bench to lunch on. He says, "It always happens when our lunch date is interrupted by a member of my staff who needs me to solve an urgent business problem. That happens often and is part of my job. But she always blows her top, yelling in four-letter words that I don't give a damn about her since I make her wait around all the time while I tend to business. It's so embarrassing. I've told her again and again to stop making a public display—it hurts me and makes my staff snicker. That's why we're here. It's got to stop or I will leave our home for good."

We asked Kate if she ever acted this way before she was married. "Always," she replied. "My mother died when I was three and my father married and divorced three times. I always felt ignored by him. I can remember the time when I was nine and he and his second wife went to a movie and left me alone. They said they would be back at 9:00 P.M., but when they didn't return on the dot I opened the window and screamed and screamed. The whole neighborhood thought I was crazy. It turned out they had stopped for a cup of coffee after the movie. That feeling I had happened so many times. I always felt that my father, whom I adored, would leave me forever if he didn't return at the time he said he would, or even if he suddenly left the room to go to the toilet without telling me."

Children learn to bond with their primary caretaker from the moment they are born. Children need love, food, and nurturing in order to survive. When the primary caregiver is absent, the child feels abandoned and cries. Eventually, the child learns to trust others for his welfare. When the primary caregiver dies, the child feels abandoned and becomes unable to trust others. It takes a long, long time for the child to develop the ability to trust again, as Kate became aware of. Sometimes therapy is the solution to help a person with their overreactions and deep feelings of abandonment.

But Kate came to counseling too late; her marriage ended because too many years of hurt in the relationship had eroded David's love for her.

## 5. The Love-Is-Competition Masquerade

In this masquerade, love means measuring up to the love one received from one's parent and finding one's partner unloving if that doesn't occur. It means unconsciously placing your partner in competition with the image of perfect love from a parent you may still have in your mind. The need to come to terms with that parental image is the unfinished business necessary to accomplish if repeated breakups in relationships are to be prevented.

Unfinished business means that you have unresolved problems from the past that were not worked on, and now those past events are disturbing the present situation. This happened to Carrie and her husband, Bob:

Carrie is a tense bank operations officer who has just turned forty. Her husband, Bob, is in his mid-forties and is a software programmer. Bob complains, "Ever since we've been married—that was five years ago—she keeps picking on me. I get the feeling from Carrie that I can't do anything right. Although I'm very successful at work, Carrie never appreciates that. She is nitpicking at me all the time. She never was that way before we were married. I don't know why she's changed. I feel like she's cutting off my balls. Maybe we should get a divorce like she's been threatening to do. You know, she's been divorced three times before—this will make it four in a row."

We then asked Carrie to tell us a bit about her parents and how she related to them when she was a child. Carrie got angry and said, "What's my childhood got to do with this? I want help now. I didn't need any help when I was a child. In fact, I had the best childhood in the world. My mother and father gave me everything, but now both are dead." She started to cry and through her tears said, "My daddy was the perfect man; he always told me I was his favorite daughter." We then asked, "Could it be possible that you have been looking for that perfect father in your husband?"

"Maybe there is a connection to my childhood after all," she said. "But no one could be as perfect as my father. That's no reason why my husband can't try to do better," she said defensively.

It was growing-up time for Carrie. But she was still demanding to be indulged by her husband, insisting he play the role of her doting father. Too many years of her self-righteousness interfered with improving her marriage with Bob. She is now looking for a fifth husband.

### 6. The Love-As-a-Commitment-Anxiety Masquerade

For many persons, love in these uncertain times becomes associated with disaster. The wonderful feeling of loving someone and being loved by that one special person becomes connected to the belief that the relationship is bound to fail; that love is simply a way station on the road to a breakup or a divorce.

We see many couples at our counseling center who are frightened to death over the fact that they love each other!

Recently, Michelle and Carl, a young couple in their mid-twenties who have never been married before, came to see us because they were on the verge of breaking up. They had been living together in an agreed-upon monogamous relationship for the past year. Things were going so smoothly that they had agreed to marry. However, three weeks before the date for their marriage their relationship turned into hell on earth, Michelle told us. At that time, Michelle found a scribbled phone number of an old girlfriend of Carl's on a piece of paper that had "accidentally" fallen in a crack in the couch.

Michelle was furious, and when she confronted Carl with this "evidence" he acknowledged he had seen this ex-girlfriend recently and gone to bed with her. "But it had nothing to do with my love for you or our getting married. It was like my last night out as a bachelor."

Michelle, on the other hand, saw it as a gross betrayal of trust: "If you do this now," she said, "what will prevent you from cheating on me after we marry? I want to find out how much you *really* love me, that's why we're here."

It turned out that Carl's "betrayal" was typical of many men and women who find themselves fearful that marriage will cause a breakup rather than enhance the love between two people. Such men and women unconsciously create a breakup before they marry to prevent them from getting even more seriously hurt after the marriage ceremony.

That happened to Carl, whose upbringing explained why: Carl's parents divorced when he was seven and he was the kid in the middle of painful divorce battles between his

Mom and Dad, which lasted for four years. As a result, he had associated getting married with getting divorced. Remembering the excruciating pain he experienced from his parents' breakup, he had unconsciously vowed that this would never happen to him when he grew up. What better way to avoid the pain of divorce than not to get married! So Carl unconsciously created a scene where he "misplaced" his ex-girlfriend's phone number where Michelle could find it. But instead of protecting himself against experiencing the "pain" of committed love, he was creating a kind of unhappiness that would haunt him the rest of his life.

Michelle could not get over her mistrust of Carl, and since neither of them were willing to forgive each other, their marriage ended before it began.

Pat and I have seen this type of commitment anxiety take place *after* a marriage occurs as well as before. It is as if a person (like Carl) were two people instead of one: a part of him (or her) values and desires a happy marriage, yet another part of that person fears the very thing he or she wants so much. Believing in the basis of their past background that what they truly want will inevitably fail to happen, they create their own divorce. Their fear has triumphed over their love.

## 7. The Love-Is-an-Implied-Bargain Masquerade

The belief that love means doing nice things for one's partner in expectation of an instant acknowledgment and return of the favor is another major misconception. Our counseling walls seem to echo with the common complaint a client will level at his or her spouse, that "You never appreciate the things I do for you."

There is, for example, John and Jeannine, married for seven years, who tell us the hurt they feel: "Like last Saturday night when we went out," John says reproachfully to Jeannine. "I went to a lot of trouble getting a good table at the restaurant you like so much, and I had a hard time getting nice seats for the play you were so eager to see afterwards. You looked so great and smelled so good, all I wanted to do was make love to you when we came home. But no, you said, 'I'm too tired, not tonight, dear.' Not even saying you had a nice time! Not even thanking me! And rejecting my hugs and kisses!"

Jeannine was shocked. "Of course I loved the evening out, but do I have to tell you how grateful I was? How many times have I gone out of my way for you without your telling me you appreciate it? I wasn't rejecting you—I really was very exhausted from all the housework I did that day, and you should have had the consideration to respect my feelings instead of getting angry with me."

John had fallen victim to his belief that love meant I-will-do-something-for-you-only-if-you-will-do-something-for-me-in-return. An offshoot of this attitude is making the fatal mistake of believing that if-my-partner-loved-me-he/she-would-know-what-I'm-thinking-and-feeling-without-my-saying-so. Love then evaporates into resentment-collecting. For love is not a commodity to be exchanged for another commodity of "equal" value. Love is not a business balance sheet where the bottom line is in red ink if you value the relationship only by what you get rather than freely give.

John is still busy today resentment-collecting, while Jeannine is now his ex-wife, who insists that for her love is a freely given gift, not a demand.

• • •

You may very well recognize you or your ex-spouse's behavior in one or more of the masquerades of love you have just read. These masquerades are major contributing causes of most divorces, giving rise to much misunderstanding, many misconceptions and lasting resentment. In our counseling sessions, we have heard hundreds of divorcing men and women complain as follows:

*"My marriage was always a win-lose proposition and my spouse always won and I always lost. He (or she) had a will of iron and always insisted on being right."*

In some marriages, "love" is seen as a contest in which one person's desire must be fulfilled at the expense of one's partner. Compromise is considered a sign of weakness and "losing." In this kind of marriage both spouses lose. There are no winners—except their lawyers in the divorce.

*"How could I show all of my true feelings to my wife? It would show I was a wimp and I'd lose her respect. Then she complained at our divorce hearing that I was cruel and unfeeling. All I was doing was trying to be strong."*

Here, "love" is equated with being a strong person, and a strong person is seen as one who never shows his or her true feelings, such as sadness, hurt, vulnerability, or fear. However, this attitude has nothing to do with authentic love. You gain love and respect when you show the entire range of who you are as a person. People marry a whole human being in a good marriage, not someone who hides a part of him or herself.

*"I thought my ex-spouse would always be kind and understanding and attentive to my needs, just like my father was. I sure was disappointed!"*

One misconception that can lead to divorce is the belief that your partner must measure up to your own kind and loving parent(s). All you can expect in a good marriage is adult love, not a parent/child kind of love. The person who always compares his or her partner to an idealized parent will never find a partner that can measure up.

*"My wife always used sex as a bargaining chip. If she thought I was a 'good boy,' I got some, and if I wasn't, it meant I didn't get any."*

Here, sex was viewed as an entitlement by the husband and as behavior control by the wife. Both were mistaking these bargaining-chip approaches for expressions of love. In a good marriage, sex is an expression of delight freely given by both spouses, of mutual respect rather than of individual desires.

*"I always wanted to be with my wife because I loved her so much. I always wanted to be at her side at parties and hated her visiting her girlfriends on her own without me. But at the time of our divorce she said I was strangling her by doing that. I showed her I loved her and she said I tried to possess and strangle her instead. How dare she!"*

The belief that "love" means possessing your spouse has nothing to do with authentic love. Instead, it is a form of separation anxiety—a feeling that your partner will leave you permanently if you don't watch him or her every minute. It is a sign of a lack of self-esteem, feeling one is not worthy of one's partner's love so that your partner will find someone better if you don't guard him/her every single waking moment.

*"My wife was getting fat, and she wasn't exercising. I told her to exercise just like I do and lose weight like I was doing. I also tried to set her thinking straight about who to vote for and what kind of hobbies she should have. I loved her so much I wanted her to be like me, but she was so ungrateful and screamed at me that I wouldn't let her be her own person."*

The mistaken belief here is the feeling that "If my partner truly loves me, she must think, feel, and act the way I do. That's because I love her so much and want the best for her." This is self-centeredness rather than love. In a good marriage, each person respects his/her partner as a separate individual, as well as part of a couple in a relationship. As separate individuals both are entitled to personal growth, which means tolerance of differences in opinion and behavior, as well as growth as a couple in terms of achieving common goals.

*"Why couldn't my spouse see I was hurting and angry at the way our marriage was going down the tubes? Instead, my spouse told me at the time I said I wanted a divorce that it came as a total surprise because he/she had seen nothing wrong in our marriage!"*

In this case, both partners were complicit in playing the mind-reading game, which is the complaint that "If you really loved me, you would know what I am thinking and believing and the reasons for my behavior without my telling you in advance." However, if we could read other people's minds and actions, we would all be millionaires! Alas, such is not the case. Love means telling your partner what you think and feel and the reasons for your actions. If a couple loves each other, they will delight in this form of communication.

*"My wife used to complain that if I really loved her, I would make more money, or take her on a cruise, or buy her a nicer house or bigger car, or whatever. I loved my wife, so I did my damnedest to give her what she wanted, but it was never enough."*

Both husband and wife made the mistake of believing that material things were an expression of love. When you believe things will give you the happiness you yearn for in a marriage, you are sinking into a bottomless pit of unhappiness instead. The way in which a couple relates to each other (kindness, empathy, tenderness, compassion, openness, etc.) is the true manifestation of love. Material things can never substitute for this kind of relationship.

Every one of our clients who made these or similar complaints had married for love, to the best of their understanding of what love meant. However, they had trapped themselves into believing that the masquerades of love they had practiced once they were married were the real thing, and holding onto those beliefs led to divorce rather than greater love. Every one of the examples quoted above is a recipe for disaster in a marriage.

• • •

We have said that a creative divorce begins with self-empowerment. No one can improve his or her life after divorce without taking personal responsibility for making positive things happen when you become single. Consequently, if you find yourself still believing in any of the love "masquerades" noted above, you must take personal responsibility for avoiding them when you begin dating again, or when you try to nurture a new relationship. Otherwise, any new relationship is likely to repeat the "dead end" of your previous marriage.

Should you see recurrences of this kind of self-defeating behavior, and you find it difficult to expunge them on your own, the healthiest and best way to overcome them is to seek out a psychotherapist who specializes in divorce-related issues, or join a divorce counseling group of men and women who are experiencing similar concerns about their relationships. In today's times, both types of help are available nationwide. All you have to do is take on the responsibility for finding them in your community.

• • •

## The True Meaning of Authentic Love

The divorces we noted above resulted from couples becoming trapped by one of the seven masquerades of love. Their divorces could have been avoided if these couples had been aware of their self-defeating actions and then wished to change them into an authentic love relationship.

Authentic love means practicing being kind teachers and receptive students to each other. It recognizes that all of us on earth are potentials in the present and future rather than finished products. Bringing out the very best in each other, validating who we are and might become is at the very heart of authentic love. We have much to learn from each other in terms of kindness, courtesy, self-improvement, and the ability to prevail over the tragedies in life as well as in the creation of our successful moments.

Divorce gives us a second chance to rethink the meaning of love and learn why the love you once thought you had forever at the time you married evaporated later on. Such love was bound to disappear since it was based on a perishable masquerade substitute for authentic love.

*Authentic love* are action words. To say to a person "I love you" is meaningless unless it is demonstrated in appropriate deeds. It means practicing the belief that you and your partner are true equals in a relationship; that you respect each other as separate individuals and also are interdependent; that you delight in and support each other's growth as separate individuals since that enhances your relationship rather than diminishing it; that your love is based on total trust, which means it is a gratuitous gift two people give to each other. In Dorothy Parker's words, "Love is like quicksilver in the hand. Leave the fingers open and it stays. Clutch it and it darts away."

If the pain of your divorce leads you to this conclusion, you will be well on your way to making your new life a creative experience instead of a rerun of the past.

# 4

# HEALTHY SEX AFTER YOUR DIVORCE

Newly divorced men and women often feel they are trapped in a time-warp now that they are free to date and have sex with whom they please. It's as if all the rules they once learned about dating and relating no longer exist:

- The wild and free divorced person, once the envy of unhappily married men and women who fantasized how exciting their sex life would be if only they were divorced, is a fantasy. Today, promiscuous one-night-stand sex has become a minefield where AIDS, chlamydia, herpes or any number of other sexual diseases may be found in the next bar a divorced person might visit.

- The old male I'll-pay-for-the-dinner-and-you'll-pay-me-back-with-sex behavior will be taken as a macho affront by the independent woman you are dating.
- Personal card exchanges at parties and the telephone calls that result from them are often initiated by women rather then men.
- My-place-or-yours? may be initiated by the woman a divorced man dates.
- In the bedroom, women are more likely to openly express their desires and needs for sexual fulfillment and act on them. They are no longer passive recipients of male "favors."
- Sexual intercourse today in the dating game involves "safe" sex, including the use of condoms and the pill. It often means a mutually agreed-upon visit to a doctor or clinic to determine whether each person is free of AIDS or any other sexual disease. Otherwise, instant sex on the first date with someone you may know slightly or not at all is playing Russian Roulette.

• • •

There is a tendency for recently divorced men and women to overvalue sexual experience because good sex is usually one of the first things to disappear in a marriage headed for a divorce. Men as well as women are "too tired" or "have a headache" or say "later, later." Or one person gets to bed earlier, the other stays up later so as not to miss a favorite TV program. . . . Excuses are endless when a marriage turns sour. Sleeping in separate beds, for example, can become the beginning of infrequent sex; many couples then have sex only once or twice a year.

In such circumstances, denial, boredom, or a lack of interest in sexual intercourse (one of our clients termed her ex-spouse's sexual attempts as "an assault with a dead weapon") tends to create the fantasy belief that sex is the most important thing in life, and the lack of it is cause for divorce. When a man or woman enters the divorce arena, both learn that the sexual encounters they can now freely engage in are most often no more than substitutes for masturbation or a quick-fix equivalent of a snort of cocaine with an unsatisfying after-effect.

"I always thought there were so many attractive men in the world that I would want to sleep with before I was divorced. Anyone, but anyone, would be better than the turkey of a husband I had," said Terri, an attractive thirty-six-year-old woman who now was fed up with the dating game. "I found out, much to my disappointment, that I was very wrong. I never knew there were so many manipulative, exploitative, and, yes, stupid men in this world. Some of them did have the capacity to give me good orgasms. But I soon learned I needed men with something more than an iron penis—I needed an intelligent person I could talk to and make love with instead of just participating in a mechanical act. I thought when I divorced all I needed was great sex to solve all my problems. How wrong I was!"

Harry is forty-one and echoes Terri's complaint from a divorced man's point of view. "When I go to a party where I don't know most of the people there, I look at it as an opportunity to meet new and interesting women. Now I'm not so sure this is right for me. Because every time I go—and I'm frequently invited by my friends—I'm disappointed. Here's what happened last week: I see this attractive woman, Claire, introduce myself, and great, she's been divorced three years like me. But it only took a minute before she was grilling me like a detective: Where did I work? What part of town did I live in? Did I have a career? What's the make of my car? Oh, she was very pleasant and smiling, but it was as if she had given me Novocaine while extracting my tooth. I wanted to find out what she was like as a person, but all she wanted to do was to find out if I was a good meal ticket.

"I find more and more women out there in the singles world exactly like Claire. I'm beginning to think it's time for me to take a rest. The next time one of my friends invites me to a party, I think I'll pass and read a good book instead. . . . And then there are the women who exploit me. Not prostitutes, just women with good jobs who use men as if they were Kleenex filled with snot. There was Lori, who was a woman I went to bed with. I thought we had good sex—she came and so did I. But then, just before dawn, she looks at the clock on the side of the bed and says 'It's four o'clock, time for you to leave.' Just like that! I had expected to spend the night—she led me to believe that—but now she was as cold as ice. It was like a business transaction in which she got what she wanted and didn't give a damn about me. Whoever said all divorced men were lucky bastards because they were free to screw anyone they wanted day and night should be put in an institution. . . . And I'm the guy who thought all my problems were over once I was divorced because my ex-wife and I had such a rotten sex life!"

• • •

In our sex-drenched culture it's normal to overvalue sex as the major cause of marital estrangement. However, recently divorced men and women soon learn that sexual problems may be 90% of a bad relationship, but it is only 10% of a good one. They learn that sex is the barometer of a relationship, rather than a cause or solution. A couple, for instance, may have what they call "great" sex regularly and still have an intolerable marriage, where sex is the quick-fix disguise of serious problems such as family violence or drug and alcohol abuse. And if caring, compassion, equal partnership, empathy, and kindness are not components of a relationship, sex as a solution to problems becomes a prime-time television illusion.

No person is immune to the imprinting of sex on our psyche since all the media in surround sight and sound becomes part of our daily cultural experience. "Sex sells" advertising agencies crow and flood us with images and innuendoes that stoke sexual desires to entice us to buy the car, the suit, the dress, the perfume, the house that have been transformed into sexual objects for credit card use. That family member, the television set, demeans the nourishing value of sex every time the family relaxes in front of the usual movie-of-the-week or sitcoms and watches bodies, that are as bare as prevailing censorship will allow, writhe in simulated sexual intercourse. And if we shield our children from this nightly fare, they escape our group to witness MTV programs that are just as sexually explicit. The fact that these programs proliferate rather than disappear in the face of many complaints is testament to the reality that millions of people continue to be attracted to and titillated by these programs and indeed buy products because of their pseudo-sexual appeal.

The discovery that sex needs to be placed in perspective in relationships rather than being the definer of the relationship ("good" sex equals good relationships, "bad" sex equals bad relationships) is one of the major revelations that can turn a newly divorced person in the direction of a creative divorce rather than a disastrous one. For that to happen, a trial run of experimenting with your new freedom is necessary. You need the cold-shower realization that sex—even good sex—is not the answer to divorce problems that lie behind the sexual curtain. Perhaps the major discovery so many recently divorced men and women make is that sex without intelligence, tenderness, empathy, sensitivity, caring, and equality of satisfying each other's needs is "Boring! Boring! Boring!" as one divorced woman practically shouted at us when talking about her disillusionment after living through a marriage in which her husband had become impotent and all she thought about was the need for sexual gratification.

To lose an illusion is painful, but to gain wisdom in its place is enormously helpful: the pain is the price that needs to be paid in order for you to move toward a bright rather than a bleak future in your new relationships.

• • •

## Making Friends with Your New Sexual Self

All men and women are sexual creatures from the time of their birth (after all, it is the excitement of sexual contact that creates us in the first place). We learn what sex means in our lives from the family in which we grew up. Our basic sexual imprint derives from the relationship of our parents since they are our entire world from which we inherit our fundamental values and behavior during the earliest years of our lives. In later years friends, career, relationships, and the enormous culture impact of TV and other media reinforce or modify what we learned in our family-of-origin years, but they never diminish the primary power of that parental conditioning. All too often what we have learned may be totally inappropriate for our own marriage, even though our parents' sexual behavior may have worked for them. The following recent example of what is really a clash of two different kinds of parental imprinting, but that was misinterpreted by both husband and wife as rejection and a loss of love, indicates how this misunderstanding, unless corrected, can lead to divorce, as it did in this case:

Toni and Brandon, both in their late twenties and in their fourth year of marriage, voiced the following complaints: Toni complained that their sexual relationship was a disaster. She said, "It used to be before we were married, Brandon couldn't take his hands off of me and we had sex every day and loved it. Now it's like I'm living with a celibate. When

I'm excited and approach him first, he usually has an excuse, like later or I'm too tired or tomorrow instead. Or, if we do go to bed, it's like I'm dragging him there just to satisfy me. And then it's over in ten seconds; he turns over to his side of the bed and goes to sleep. But if he wants it, which isn't often, he's ticked off at me if I don't drop my pants and immediately get it on with him. I feel I'm being rejected all the time."

On the other hand, Brandon felt threatened when his wife took the first step in initiating sex. "It's as if she's cutting off my balls," he said. "I don't like aggressive women; it's like they're attacking me. So my penis shrinks, and I do feel tired when Toni insists on jumping my bones. But, it's a funny thing. I don't feel that way at all when I feel the urge and start grabbing Toni first."

It turned out that their dissatisfaction with each other's behavior was based on a clash of two cultures that was resulting in a loss of love. When Brandon was growing up he never saw his mother take the initiative in hugging or kissing his father. It was always his father who made the first move. "My mom was always there for me as my mom, but she took a back seat to Dad. He always made the important decisions," Brandon said. What Brandon saw in his family was that being manly was being the initiator, making all the major family decisions. He had unconsciously connected his own sense of self-esteem to being the initiator, and that spilled over into his concept of how sexual relationships should be in married life.

On the other hand, Toni grew up in a household where she was told by her mother, "Become someone; don't just be a housewife. Make a life for yourself; have a good career as well as a nice family. I love your father, but I regret leaving college and giving up my desire to become an interior decorator in order to marry him. That was the times, but you have opportunities I never had. Go for them."

She had indeed incorporated her mother's philosophy into her own sense of self-worth. She had completed her B.A. in college and was thinking of getting an M.B.A. This sense of self-assertiveness became ingrained in her from her mother and also was wholeheartedly reinforced by her father.

It was Brandon's perception of himself that believed Toni, the person he had loved the most, would think less of him as a man, would regard him as a wimp, if he were the passive recipient of her sexual initiatives. On the other hand, Toni regarded her self-assertiveness as an enhancement of her sexual attractiveness rather than its negation.

After his divorce, Brandon continued to come to us for counseling. He learned that he had been struggling with Toni in a misguided way "to protect his manhood" as he called it. He had defined his sense of himself as a person of value and worth by his sexual behavior rather than by the whole person he was. He had been unconsciously unaware of the power of his family upbringing on the way he defined himself sexually. When this was brought to his attention, Brandon told us he was shocked to discover how much he was, in his terms, "victimized" by his past family upbringing. "I always thought I was an up-to-date guy, always believed Toni and I were equals and that being macho was stupid. I've read all the new books and articles on how to practice sex today and how different it is from my mom and dad's time. But boy, you just don't get over your upbringing by only being intellectual about it. It's been stamped in my soul without my knowing it, and it's a good thing that now I'm aware of why I was acting the way I did.

"It's sad that I didn't know this while I was married to Toni, but she was as stubborn as I was. What I now know is I'll never be trapped in my old ways again."

Understanding their families' sexual past instead of repeating it will make people like Brandon move in the direction of a creative divorce rather than wallowing in past regrets and anger. There are millions of other couples like Brandon and Toni who find themselves experiencing sexual incompatibilities based on their parental imprinting. Their backgrounds may be different from Brandon's and Toni's, but their sexual relationship similarly becomes a problem rather than a delight because they, too, are unconsciously echoing their parents' way of relating, no matter how "modern" they think they are.

Our fundamental attitudes and behavior about sex are learned from our parents. They are the first and therefore the most important and powerful teachers of the way in which we will engage in sexual relationships when we grow up. But what we have learned from our parents aren't always appropriate guidelines for our own relationships. In fact, some of these learned experiences may prove detrimental and be a major contributing cause of divorce, as in the case of Toni and Brandon.

Since you are now thinking about or engaging in new sexual relationships after your divorce, it is possible to gain new insight into your sexual upbringing and personality and to use this self-knowledge to develop better relationships and have better sex now that you are single. Indeed, healthy sexual attitudes and behavior are essential elements for a creative divorce. The next section discussed the major variations of dysfunctional parental imprinting that place people on the road to divorce.

• • •

## The Twelve Major Dysfunctional Parental Imprints

### 1. The My-Sexual-Partner-Is-My-Permanent-Entertainment-Industry Imprint

Growing up in a family where one's parents, usually a father, believes it is his "right" to have sex when he wants it, regardless of the feelings of his spouse, imprints the feeling of sexual entitlement in a son. This means no consideration is given to one's partner's needs and any sign of resistance to his instant gratification is then misread as a lack of love. The stage is then set for a resentment-collecting marriage.

### 2. The Passive-Aggressive-Sex-Dance Imprint

Women who saw their mother resent the self-centered, selfish sexual behavior of their father but never directly confront him, will tend to replicate their mother's behavior in their own marriage. The resentment becomes expressed indirectly (for example, going on a credit card binge, which angers the husband, or the I'm-too-tired-and-besides-it's-my-PMS-time "getting even" approach).

## 3. The I-Am-My-Penis Imprint

This is the father who has always bragged about his sexual prowess: the great size of his penis and its rod-of-steel ability to sustain an erection. All of his sense of self-esteem is focused on the one thing where he feels he's the winner. He may have a low salary in a demeaning job and feel exploited by his boss, but at least he can feel "important" because of his sexual power.

If the son feels similarly trapped in a dead-end job and has little self-esteem, he, too, may have a tendency to feel good about himself only if his spouse (and the friends he always tells about the duration and frequency of his sexual activities) validates his sexual prowess. This self-centeredness and personal insecurity can turn into anxiety, self-hatred, and despair when in the normal process of aging (forty is not seventeen!) his sexual ability diminishes.

## 4. The Sex-As-Violence Imprint

There is the tendency to mistake sex for a form of abuse when a child witnesses parents' screaming and physically hitting each other as a prelude to "resolving" their fight by going to bed and "making love." The excitement of the battle is used as a stimulus for sexual excitement.

Only recently, Clint, a twenty-five-year-old man married for one year, told us he saw no reason why his wife Dana insisted on coming to see us. "Sure, I hit her when she doesn't agree with me, and I yell, trying to convince her how wrong she is. I get real charged up and the sex is great that night," he said.

Clint was surprised to find out that there were better ways to have a good sexual relationship. Physical abuse and sex do not go together like a horse and carriage. "But doesn't every one? I saw it happen in my parents' home all the time," he asked us.

Everyone doesn't, we answered.

### 5. The Sexual Promiscuity Imprint

In this case, the alcoholic, barfly father is always prone to coming home late to the now-cold dinner mom prepared, smelling of another woman's perfume. The son, seeing his mother's pain, vows that when he grows up and marries he will never become an alcoholic. But the stresses in his life as a grownup have proven too great, and he, too, drifts into an alcoholic lifestyle and one-night stands while his wife fumes.

When he comes to us for counseling, he is surprised to discover that he has become the very person he did not want to be. He is also surprised to find out that there was a genetic predisposition to alcoholism in his family of origin and that he could not control his drinking. If he still refuses to stop drinking as the first step in repairing the rift in his relationship with his wife, their marriage will be a thing of the past.

### 6. The I'm-Going-to-Be-the-Exact-Sexual-Opposite-of-My-Parents Imprint

Children view things in black and white. Often a son or a daughter, seeing their parents relate in sexually incompatible ways, may determine to be the exact opposite when he/she grows up. So a daughter may become uninhibited sexually when she grows up, since she saw how her mother found sex a burden rather than a pleasure. "It was like she felt assaulted all the time," Jan, a client, told us. She also said, "I was determined to explore sex as pleasure and get as much of it as I could, not like my mother. I thought that was the answer, but I'm here in counseling because I found it is not making me happy. My short-term affairs more and more feel like a waste of time, like I've seen one guy, I've seen them all."

Paradoxically, in trying to be the exact opposite of her mother, she was really being controlled by her mother. For her mother's behavior determined her own behavior: she was thinking in childlike, black-and-white terms, telling herself, "Since my mother's behavior is 'black' (wrong behavior), my doing exactly the opposite will be 'white' (right behavior)."

What Jan neglected to realize was that neither her mother's behavior nor its opposite was the right choice. She had to define her own personal sexual identity without unconsciously using her mother's experience as the major influence in reversed form. The behavior she thought was opposite from her mother's resulted in the same kind of feeling that sex was indeed a burden to be endured!

### 7. The Sex-Is-a-Let's-Make-a-Deal Imprint

There are the parents who transformed sexual behavior into a businesslike transaction: the wife would withhold sexual favors until the husband agreed to fulfill a desire of hers that he otherwise would have refused. It could be the new expensive dress she wanted or a preferred vacation spot or getting a better house or a pricey furniture set she longed for.

Seeing that mother is successful imprints on a daughter's mind that sex is a manipulative device designed to exact from men their agreement to give her what they ordinarily would refuse. Not only does this result in coy sparring matches, but it can also become a way of life where one's self-esteem becomes dependent on using sex as a favor to give or withhold. Marilyn Monroe, for example, seemed to feel that she was a person of value and worth not for who she was but for the sexual favors people desired from her, which intensified her depression and suicidal impulses.

## 8. The Sex-Is-a-Guilty-Pleasure Imprint

There are the deeply religious parents whose religion taught them that having sex simply for pleasure rather than procreation was a sin. This belief was reinforced by their never talking about sex to their children or demonstrating behavior such as hugging or kissing in front of them. The children would gather that something was exciting but also wrong when they would hear bumps, squeaks, muffled screams, and laughter from their parents' bedroom long after their parents believed they were asleep. A peculiar form of warfare seemed to be going on between mom and dad.

Growing up under these conditions can give rise to a guilty pleasure sexual syndrome. This can create considerable anxiety and confusion in one's partner if one sends out mixed sexual feelings where pleasure is laced with guilt. For example, when Tom and Candyce, who say they love each other and want to marry, came to see us, Candyce said only one thing stood in the way. "Our sex life is so exasperating," she said. "When we make love it's great, but it only happens a couple of times a month, but if I had my way it would happen every day. And a funny thing happens every time he comes: he has to get out of bed immediately and take a shower. It destroys all the warm feelings I could have. I want to cuddle and be hugged after intercourse. Oh, how I hate those showers he takes!"

Tom said he felt compelled to take those showers after an orgasm but didn't know why. He also had intense sexual desires towards Candyce, but somehow felt he could only perform a couple of times a month, using as the excuse that he may not have enough sperm to satisfy her more often. What was really occurring inside of Tom's psyche was a war between his desire for sexual pleasure and his feeling very guilty if indeed he did desire it, remembering his parents' injunction that sex without procreation is sinful. He compromised unconsciously by permitting himself to enjoy sex infrequently, as if to say he was really not such a sinful person after all. And the shower was always present and necessary to wash away his guilt symbolically when he actually did have intercourse. Only when he comes to terms with these self-created demons will sex become an unconditional enhancement of their love for each other. Otherwise, Tom and Candyce will divorce before they ever marry.

## 9. The Sex-Is-a-Triangle Imprint

This is the family in which mother played favorites. Not feeling love toward her husband, she would tend to unconsciously treat her first-born son as a surrogate husband—as an adult love-object rather than demonstrating appropriate mother-child love. The son receives confusing double messages: he yearns to be loved as the child he is, but is also receiving the message that he is the substitute husband in his mother's eyes. He may then view himself as a rival to his father for his mother's love, creating a conflict inside himself, which if not resolved in adulthood would doom him to relive this imagined triangle in his mind in any new love relationship he tries to establish. He will repetitively create a triangular sexual relationship whenever he tries to establish a monogamous relationship. A sexual commitment to one person exclusively feels dangerous to him because at the unconscious level he feels he has "won" his mother at the expense of his father. That is an intolerable feeling, for a child doesn't want to "win" his mother and dispose of his father. What he really wants is the unconditional love of *both* of his parents, which has been denied him. To escape the "danger" of monogamous sex, the grownup son will, when married, create a triangle through extramarital sex. Unless he comes to terms with the child-based terror that he is the antagonist of his father for his mother's love, there will always be a third party present when he has sex with a person he believes he loves; that party is the mother-in-his-mind telling him, "You can only love me, so stop being unfaithful with someone else."

When he is aware that this fantasy is controlling his life, he can then have a real monogamous marriage instead of creating serial divorces because of his affairs.

## 10. The Caretaker Sexual Imprint

This is the daughter who has been singled out to become the surrogate adult when a mother or father is seriously incapacitated or dies when she hasn't even reached the puberty stage. The child, burdened with the demands of keeping the household functioning, learns to believe she is only valued for the help she gives others. She is unassertive about her own needs and ultimately begins to believe she is not even entitled to express her own needs, let alone have them fulfilled. For example, Clara, an attractive never-married freelance writer in her early forties, tells us, "My mother had leukemia when I was nine years old and my brother was only five. It was an illness that lasted eight years before she died. I was obligated to take over most of her household duties. I was always praised for being 'momma's great helper.' It still rings in my ears, dad telling me this all the time. . . . I never thought I was really very sexy; all I knew was that I had to take care of my loved ones who desperately needed my help. I've always been sexually attracted to broken-wing men, those you would call helpless or losers. My last live-in partner, Corbin, was unemployed for two years, and I supported him all that time. Before him it was Norman, who when I let him use my credit card ran up a five-thousand-dollar debt that I'm still paying off. And now I'm attracted to a guy who looks good, but I'm scared to death of getting into another mess. People tell me I'm good-looking, but I never believe them. Does that mean I don't believe any man in my life really wants me, but only what I can do for him?

She asked the right question. Her sense of who she was as a woman and her sexual self were based on the belief that she was a wonderful caretaker and service industry to others. Consequently, she only felt sexually valuable if she could fulfill her partner's sexual needs rather than her own, even when she knew they were unreasonable or hurtful. When she learned that she had every right to experience delight in her own sexuality and that the man in her life should be responsive to her needs also, her new relationship turned into the best one she ever had. "I still feel it's good to be a caregiver, but not at the expense of who I am and what I want for myself. It's nice to know as I do now that I can truly think of myself as sexually attractive," she told us on a recent visit.

### 11. The Sex-As-Incest Imprint

There is no more devastating assault on a child's personality, self-esteem, and sexuality than experiencing incest by a parent or a close relative. Young daughters (or stepdaughters) are the primary victims. It has been estimated that as many as one in three women have been sexually abused in childhood, usually by the person that child trusts and loves most. That daughter can grow up into an adult who mistrusts the world and sees herself as a helpless sexual victim because men only exist to dominate women. Sex appears to such a woman as a throwaway item, a pawn in a power relationship. Tenderness, hugging, and mutually consenting sex are unknowns; manipulative sex as a survival technique combined with chronic depression become the only sexual reality. Because our society has now spotlighted incest as a problem to be solved rather than a shame to be hidden, new hope exists for the women (and men) who have suffered incest to become the loving sexual individuals they always hoped to be. Incest survivors' groups, abuse hotlines, psychological counseling, and legal actions are now available aids toward a better life.

### 12. The Sex-As-a-Substitute-for-Love Imprint

As sexual human beings we are the personal manufacturers of our sexual dreams, hopes, and desires. We can either use this enormous freedom to elicit the best qualities inherent in our nature or the worst. The healthy human desire to expand sexual fusion into a validation on the physical level of the love two people may feel for each other can become misdirected as a result of the parental imprintings we have examined above.

Sex in these circumstances becomes a substitute for love rather than its physical expression. The person who has grown up in a family where rage and violence is associated with the sexual act will label that rage and violence an expression of love: giving a spouse a black eye is considered a "love tap" rather than the physical assault it is. The woman who allows herself to be mistreated sexually will label that mistreatment "love." The man who seeks out one-night stands while he is married may believe the self-deception that he has an overabundance of sexual energy that when released with women outside the marriage makes him more loving toward his wife. The person who always feels compelled to ask after intercourse, have I satisfied you? may be expressing performance anxiety and labeling it love for his partner. The woman who fakes orgasms and is fearful of telling her partner what pleasures her sexually may call that "love for my spouse" when it is an expression of her low self-esteem. The rapist will claim that his sexual attacks are a sign of his overpowering love for women when it really is an unconscious act of rage and hatred of women. The man who "overpowers" his wife when all she wants is to be left alone may claim he is expressing his "manly love" for his wife, when really he is committing an act of self-centered aggression. His feel-good dominance masquerades as love.

Our attitudes about sexuality and its meaning in our lives, of course, are tremendously shaped and reinforced by the culture in which we live. Mindless copulations, implying that instant gratification and orgasmic potency are the only meaning sex has in life, are the daily fare of television programs, films, and the news media that consider sex scandals their daily bread.

This kind of cultural conditioning has an insidious effect on one's psyche since we are constantly and repetitively brainwashed into believing self-centered sex based solely on instant pleasure for oneself to the exclusion of one's partner's desires is the only kind of sex that's worthwhile. "Jumping one's bones," "getting it on," words which are frequently used as shorthand terms for sexual intercourse, are the giveaway expressions of this trivialization of the sexual experience.

A survey of how our culture has defined our sexual selves in the past three decades can help us move beyond this straitjacketing of our capacity to make sex an enhancement of love rather than its negation. For there is light at the end of the sexual tunnel, since a more mature understanding of the spiritual meaning of sex in our lives has been evolving in our culture over the past thirty years and exists side-by-side with the bombardment of uncaring sex expressed in today's media.

• • •

## The Thirty-Year Journey Toward Meaningful Sexuality

The enormous changes that have taken place in our society over the past thirty years as a result of the microchip revolution are paralleled by equally dramatic changes in society's sexual attitudes during this period in time. We have moved from the naive '60s, when orgasms and sexual gymnastics were seriously proposed as solutions to the world's problems, to today's times when a more realistic, complex, and healthier understanding of the role sex plays in love and relationships exists.

In order to find your way in the dramatically changed sexual landscape of our turn-of-the-millennium culture, you need to understand just how radically things have changed. Otherwise, you may find yourself repeating the sexual frustrations, illusions, and disappointments that so many divorced men and women complain about as contributing factors in their own divorce.

"Those who cannot remember the past are condemned to repeat it," observed the great American philosopher George Santayana. For this reason, it's critical to understand the roller-coaster attitudes about sex that have prevailed in our society over the past thirty years. In learning from the past, you can create a new, more joyful, more fulfilling sex life for yourself—this is the opportunity a creative divorce provides.

The past three decades have seen major changes in the way we view the role of sex in relationships. The decades were experimental laboratories that were created by the sexual revolution, a consequence of the invention of the pill, the new acknowledgment of women's desire for and intense enjoyment of sex (something women always knew, being multiorgasmic, but had to hide in a male-dominated culture), and the advent of frank discussions about all aspects of the sexual experience heralded by the TV talk shows. Sexual behaviors that were once considered dirty little secrets (e.g., oral sex, anal sex, homosexuality, promiscuity, group sex, masturbation, safer sex with condoms, AIDS and other sexual diseases, premature ejaculation, impotency) are now talked about as openly as talk of the weather. These changes occurred because the 1950s traditional value sexual guidelines no longer worked. Inherent in the '50s sexual attitudes was a considerable amount of hypocrisy: women could not express their sexual needs except by innuendo to husbands who all too often could not get their message, men were supposed to know how to act in bed, except that more often than not men *didn't* know; sexual positions other than the missionary position were considered obscene and often subject to legal punishment; sexual dysfunctions were not talked about, and marital counseling to remedy sexual problems was nonexistent.

The new sexual openness that appeared in the '60s was liberating and valuable in the sense that it focused attention on the urgent need for a new and better kind of sexual relationship between the sexes. But since there was no consensus on what new sexual values had to be substituted for the old ones, each subsequent decade whirled around from one extreme to another to find answers that would make for happy marriages. For example:

- If you were married in the '60s, sexual behavior was presented by the culture of that time as a science to be mastered, courtesy of Masters and Johnson and complicated graphs. Sex was an expression of noncommitment, since multiple affairs were supposed to spice up a boring marriage. Orgasms were promoted as the solution to all world problems with a seriousness that can only promote a smile today. Do drugs and you will have good sex was the theme of the times. But the drugs transformed marriages into nightmares.
- If you were married in the '70s, sexual behavior became defined as a playground, with *The Joy of Sex* the required educational text. Self-gratification and uncaring impulsiveness were trumpeted as alternatives to long-lasting monogamous relationships (since the conventional wisdom of the time affirmed the impossibility of happy, long-term relationships).
- If you were married in the late '80s-early '90s, sex became equated with disease control, with condoms,

phone sex, and X-rated videotapes becoming the safety nets. Sex as a potential AIDS threat, mixed with the urgent need for sexual gratification, hovered like a black cloud over relationships.

- Today's culture is beginning to emphasize equal partnership sex that is monogamous, AIDS-conscious and spiritual. It is sex in the context of pleasing your mate which results in further pleasure for yourself. It is sex that is experienced in an environment of friendship, empathy, caring, and kindness where actual intercourse is the fulfillment of this context rather than a substitute for it. Sex then becomes the celebration of a loving couple's soulful relationship with each other.

In today's times, we have filtered out the sand-in-the-eyes sexual experiments of the past three decades. It turns out that the best of the "old-fashioned" family values were not irrelevant after all. Indeed, they are essential for the perpetuation of a long-lasting, loving marriage, for there is the need for *unconditional trust* in each other as the essential glue required to sustain a long-lasting, loving marital relationship. And unconditional trust can only be earned by being *monogamous*. Trust and monogamy, two old-fashioned concepts that are not old-fashioned at all. Monogamy today, however, must be based on free choice, not on lip service. For in the past, monogamy has too often been honored in the breach: verbal assertions of fidelity with fingers crossed. Practicing monogamy out of free choice because one knows it is the only way to obtain the total trust of your partner, and vice versa, is a recognition that nothing will destroy a relationship as much as promiscuity will. Trust is shattered (far more than was believed to be the case in the past) when one's partner or oneself has an affair. In this time of AIDS and many other sexual diseases, the risk from promiscuity becomes an even more threatening destroyer of relationships. To acknowledge and accept the trade-off of monogamy in place of transitory sexual excitement through affairs is to validate a marriage at its deepest caring level. Our knowledge of how we can pleasure ourselves and each other is infinitely greater today than it was in our parents' time—and in that knowledge, sex with one permanent partner can become an ever-renewable, passionate series of events in which sex in the bedroom need not become sex in the bored-room.

The spiritual component of the sexual experience is also a central value that today's times reaffirm as essential to an enriching relationship. When two people experience sex in the context of pleasing your mate as well as yourself, when both feel free to openly express their sexual needs to each other, and when it is enveloped in an environment of friendship, empathy, caring, and kindness, sex becomes the soulful celebration of a loving couple's happy relationship instead of a substitute for it.

When divorced men and women break through the circle of repeating their old sexual habits now that they have the opportunity to relearn from their past, they can begin to make friends with their new sexual self—a self that creates a future which will enhance any new relationship rather than destroy it.

# 5

# PRACTICING FAIRNESS: THE PATHWAY TO A CREATIVE DIVORCE

In today's times something new and very important is occurring in divorce: more women than men are initiating divorce proceedings. The old male prerogative of taking divorce actions first (men in their own estimation being the sole determiner of whether or not a marriage stays together) has become a quaint artifact. Today's woman, insisting on being treated as an equal in her marriage, will no longer tolerate indefinitely what she considers very unfair treatment by her spouse and therefore finds no remedy other than divorce possible.

Most husbands reel under such assertiveness. We get more calls from men than women these days, telling us that "out of a clear blue sky" their wife told them she wanted a divorce. And such men often say to us, "And I thought we had a good marriage, but she tells me she's been unhappy for years." They seek our help to sort out their dilemma and puzzlement and helplessness in the face of their shock that the woman, rather than the man, is the decision-maker. It's as if they feel stripped of their manhood.

Why are women so concerned about being treated unfairly in their marriage? And why is this issue of fairness versus unfairness in marriage so significant that it leads to so many divorces? Answering these questions can help both men and women who are either thinking about divorce or who are currently in the divorce process learn some of the most important lessons about why their marriages deteriorated and how they can avoid repeating those behaviors which led to that end. And for those who have been divorced already for more than a few years, but find themselves in one frustrating relationship after another, new knowledge about these issues may help them end their frustration.

Fairness and unfairness in relationships are issues dear to Pat's heart. She is committed to equality in all phases of relationships and is sensitized to the profound effect equal treatment, or the lack of such treatment, has on women's lives. Based on her years of counseling women of all ages in all phases of their relationships, here are her answers to the questions about fairness and unfairness that we raised above:

I personally am convinced—Pat says—that for women the ultimate value in marriage is living with the person one loves on the basis of mutual consideration and equitable treatment. This means a deep-rooted confidence that the relationship is grounded in a sense of justice, a recognition that the inevitable problems that arise in any committed relationship will be justly resolved in the best interest of both parties. That best interest means there are no "winners" or "losers" when differences are resolved. For winning or losing implies that marriage is a series of battles and power struggles. That may very well be true in the business world (how many times have we heard words like "I got the deal; I killed the competition," or "It's a jungle out there"). On the other hand, marriage is not a killing ground but a continuous series of shared life experiences that offer the possibility of two people helping each other grow for the better as separate individuals and as a couple. That means eliciting the best human qualities from each other, not the worst. Otherwise, marriage becomes a form of exploitation and selfishness, which can be the consequence of believing the relationship is grounded in unfairness—the belief that one person is being taken unfair advantage of by the other.

As a woman, I can immediately empathize with the women I see in counseling who are so very much concerned about fairness—and the lack of it—in their marriage. The reality of our history as a nation has been from its very beginning the reality that women have indeed been seen as second-class citizens: women were denied the right to vote until 1920 and were defined as housewives, mothers, and caretakers, but never as career persons, until the women's movement began changing that state of affairs. It is sobering to be reminded that the issue of women's belief in the essential unfairness in the relationship between men and women dates back to before the Constitution was written. It was Abigail Adams, who would become the wife of a U.S. president and mother to another, who proclaimed in a widely publicized letter to her husband in 1776 that women resented "the tyranny of husbands" and that "If particular care and attention is not paid to the ladies, we are determined to foment a rebellion. . . ."

The dictionary defines "fairness" as "equitable treatment," which means feeling you have been treated justly. But what may be considered "fair" (or taken for granted as if it were fair) in one generation may not be considered fair by a different generation. For example, the contrast between the baby-boom generation and their parents' generation's concepts of fairness is strikingly different. In the 1950s when the baby boomers had not yet reached puberty, their parents' concept of fairness in marriage and family life meant the husband went to work and was the sole wage earner, while the wife confined herself to being housewife, mother, and nurturer of her husband. Beyond being valued as wife and mother, a woman had no validation of being a valued person in her own right. She was supposed to bask in the glory of her husband's career. All major money decisions were made by the husband, the wife being "given" a household allowance, which she had to ask for. The phrase proudly asserted at that time was that the husband was "king of his castle," with barely a mention of his wife.

This stereotyped image was accepted by society at large at that time as the "only" fair way for a marriage to exist. Equality then meant the "fair" relationship of a husband bringing in the entire income from the "outside" world, while the wife, in exchange for giving up her right to an equal voice in decision-making, was supposed to be content with the economic security and status her hard-working spouse gave her.

The advent of the women's movement and the giant cultural and economic changes of the subsequent decades have created a one-hundred-eighty degree change in this concept of fairness. Today fairness for women means equal employment opportunities in the working world outside the home; no sexual harassment on the job; both husband and wife are employed in all types of careers and jobs; marriage is an equal partnership, with the husband and wife mutually sharing household chores, and the husband is presumed to be an active partner in the birthing of the children and in caring for the children. All major decisions in the family are to be mutually discussed and arrived at in partnership.

It is my observation that we as women still have a long way to go to experience today's concept of fairness. More often than not, this principle is honored in the breach rather than reality, giving rise to much unnecessary conflict and resentment-collecting in modern marriage. In place of fairness, unfairness predominates, according to the many women I see in counseling. Here are examples of the kind of complaints women typically voice:

## The Seven Major Types of Unfairness

### 1. The Unfairness of Unequal Sharing of Household Duties

"Art always gives me a martyr's look when I ask him to pick up his shorts and socks when he gets ready for bed," says Julie with an exasperated sigh. "'What's the big deal if you pick them up?' he tells me. Well, it *is* a big deal because it's a sign of his not caring, of being selfish. 'Besides,' he says, 'don't I put the kids to bed every night? Fair is fair.' His idea of taking care of our two children—they are six and seven years old—is to play games for fifteen minutes and kiss them goodnight. 'You're home all day, with all the time in the world, while I'm busting my butt at the office, so why should I do more?' When he says that I'm ready to kill him," Julie tells me. "I patiently tell him what I do before he comes home every night, like this: I get up at 6:00 A.M., and I feed the children breakfast; I take them to school; I come back home and put a load of dirty laundry in the washing machine; then usually the bathrooms have to be cleaned and it's just about time to vacuum the whole house. And then it's time to pick the children up and I have to go to the grocery store; then the car needs gas, so I'm over to the gas station. I pick the children up at 2:00 P.M.; I help them with their homework. Now it's 3:00 P.M., so I'm starting to fix dinner. I then take out the clothes I washed and put a new load in the machine. The kids start squabbling so I run over to break up what might have turned into a fight. The kids might look at a favorite TV program which gives me a chance to sort out the bills and pay them. I'm constantly going until Art comes home. I could go on and on but I'll stop here. And Art has the nerve to say I've had all the free time in the world! Jane, my eldest, said to me yesterday, 'You know, mom, you're Cinderella. You do all the work!' I recently read about a woman who said that when she does 50 percent of the housework and caring for the kids it's considered not enough, but when her husband does 50 percent, he's considered a hero. Well, that's the story of my life too."

## 2. The Unfairness of "Betrayals"

"I feel you betrayed me; it's unfair." Greg is accusing Paula, his wife of eleven years, of going back on her word that she would never have a child. They married when both were twenty-five and agreed to never have children. Now at thirty-six, Paula feels a powerful urge to have a child and Greg instead is accusing her of being a liar. "I wasn't lying when I agreed not to have a child. I've changed since then, but that's not lying," Paula said. "You men are lucky. You can have children at ninety, but not women—my time clock is running out. What's so strange about my wanting a child now that I already have a good career and want to experience another part of myself, being a mother? And I want to see it be *our* child, no science-fiction embryo implant."

Any husband who considers this change in a woman's attitude toward having children as a "betrayal" of the marriage rather than as a profound desire to experience parenthood, which from her point of view would enhance the marriage rather than destroy it, is misreading their relationship and may destroy it.

## 3. The Unfairness of the I-Make-More-Money-Than-You Power Relationship

This is a carryover of the '50s version of the man as king-of-his-castle approach to marriage. But it can be a new variation on this old attitude. Now it can also be the situation in which the wife makes more money than the husband. This can stir up a sense of worthlessness in the husband. There is the case of Shelley who makes double the salary of her husband, Jeff. They are a "modern" couple who agree in principle that their relationship should be an equal partnership. Jeff gives lip service to the idea that this disparity in salaries doesn't matter and has told Shelley how happy he is for her success. But he defines success in terms of how much money he earns, so he considers himself a failure in Shelley's eyes. Shelley does not believe she is better than Jeff because she earns more money: the emotional bonding they have is the most important aspect of their relationship as far as she is concerned. Jeff doesn't share his feelings with Shelley but acts out his mistaken belief that she thinks less of him because of his lower salary. He starts to sulk around the house, procrastinates about doing his share of the housework, and becomes sharp-tongued by interpreting Shelley's suggestions for helping her as criticism of himself. The stage is set for a contest of wills that can and often does lead to a divorce if not corrected in time through more open communication and counseling.

### 4. The Unfairness of the Home-Is-Where-the-Heart-Isn't Relationship

Both Wendy and Steve work and like what they are doing; they pool their income but have small separate accounts that they agreed to spend without being accountable to each other; they both wanted children and have two daughters now, nine and twelve years old, whom they are bringing up to believe they can accomplish any goals they set their minds to, just like mom. However, there is one major problem: Steve is the man who is never home. It has nothing to do with his being promiscuous. To the contrary, their relationship always has been monogamous. But now Wendy says she is on the brink of a breakup of their fourteen-year marriage.

"Steve is in construction work, so his hours are erratic," she says. "I've always accepted that fact and worked around it. The trouble is that he *could* rearrange his time so he could be home more regularly and the children would know they have a father rather than an occasional visitor. And over the years he's been spending more and more of his time with his buddies—they go on fishing trips together, and then there's the two-week-every-year hunting trip. That leaves me and the children with leftovers. He's never around enough to really be part of the family. The last straw happened last week when he said, out of the blue, he was going on a fishing trip with his buddies next month because the airplane company had an extra-special inexpensive deal then. And I had plans for all of us to go on vacation together at that time! Now Steve is telling me it would be unfair to his buddies if he canceled the trip. What about his being unfair to me and the children?"

There are many men, and Steve is one of them, who unconsciously feel home life is a personal threat rather than a place of comfort, security, and fulfillment. They usually grew up in a family where violent fights occurred, where one parent often disparaged the other, and where they as little children never experienced the love and caring attention from their parents that they yearned for. Because this happened, they made surrogate families for themselves out of friendships with others. They valued these friendships more than they valued their home life and would spend as much time as possible in outside activities with them, making excuses for not being home when they were supposed to be. Out of complete unawareness, they then replicate this behavior in their own marriage to the detriment of their own family relationships. Divorce is at the end of their marriage road if this pattern of behavior never changes.

## 5. The Unfairness of Losing One's Sense of Self

Joan is aghast: "I've become a corporate man's wife, just like my mother! And I swore this would never happen to me," she said. "Both of my parents died when I was fifteen. I grew up in a wealthy family that traveled around the world because of my father's being an international bank manager. I always had a nanny, but what I really wanted was my mother's warmth and love. But she gave that—and her soul—to my father. He demanded that she be the perfect corporate executive's hostess. Most of the social gatherings they had were because dad believed they were good for business. When they died in a car crash, they died without a penny to their name. They had lived far beyond their means, but it turned out my not having any money was a good thing. It made me rely on my own resources, and since I had a talent for interior decorating, I went to college and majored in art and developed an independent practice as a decorating consultant. I had escaped the trap that happened to so many of my friends: they became trust-fund babies who never had to stretch themselves to get a career and work hard at it. They became soft, self-indulgent, and not very happy. They didn't feel very good about themselves, since they never earned the money they had inherited. It was just an accident of their birth.

"At the time I met Giorgio five years ago, I was pretty happy with myself as an independent woman in a job I had created and liked. A real 1990s woman! But it was also the time I felt ready for marriage. I was thirty-three and began to feel the need for creating a family, but not like the one I came from. I was a lonely only child starved for love. I wanted a loving husband who would be "there" for me, and also at least two children who would get the attention from me that I never got from my parents. Giorgio seemed to be the man of my dreams. He was forty-five, charismatic, charming, a self-made man, the head of a successful New York-based cosmetics firm, so sweet and attentive when he was courting me. When we married three years ago, I gave up my business, which was on the West Coast, and moved to New York to be with him. There was no need to have a business three thousand miles away from him, and I could always rebuild my consulting practice in New York, Giorgio told me. It sounded reasonable, and he said there would be no problem in my getting consulting jobs in New York because his influential friends would help me.

"Little did I know. It's turned out that Giorgio is completely self-centered and wants me only as his ornament. I want none of that. I feel like I'm duplicating my mom's life. I'm the hostess for his business parties, and he wants me at the snap of his fingers to travel with him to places like Spain, France, and Italy to relieve his boredom on the trips. I'm not impressed with trips—traveling of any kind. I had too many plane trips growing up. I'm also broke, because when I gave up my consulting practice I also gave up my income. Giorgio has not lived up to his promise to connect me with his influential friends to establish a career for myself in New York. He always has an excuse not to do so, but I really think he doesn't want me to have any independence because that might interfere with his need for me to be with him on the many business trips he makes every year. He says these long trips are boring without me.

"I'm dependent on his handouts for any spending money and it makes me feel like I'm worthless. I've lost most of the self-respect I had and I'm very angry at Giorgio. Oh yes, he says having two children would be no problem, but I can just see my kids duplicating what happened to me as a child—there would be nannies for them while I became the perfect hostess and traveling companion for Giorgio. My mom would be turning in her grave, because I knew how much she hated that kind of life. Yet here I am becoming my mother!"

In the 1950s, Joan's mother's time, the issue of nurturing one's sense of self was nonexistent. Of course, society and the culture of the '50s told her she had the best of all possible worlds. For she could bask in the glory of her husband's success and enjoy his status and income. You can't be more fortunate than that, the values of her time proclaimed. Unhappily, Joan's mother accepted that conditioning without question and felt she "shouldn't" be unhappy! In fact, she felt she had no right to be unhappy, yet Joan saw her looking sad and weepy most of the time.

On the other hand, Joan has been conditioned by society to believe a woman's self-worth and self-respect are an absolute necessity for leading a fulfilling life. When that sense of self and self-respect is undermined or attacked, women such as Joan will fight to prevent it from happening. For Joan, the issue has become clear cut: Giorgio must acknowledge her needs as well as his own. And if he continues to treat her as his appendage, rather than as a person in her own right, she is prepared to leave the marriage. "After all," she says, "I know I can survive on my own. I love Giorgio and want to avoid a breakup, but I'm not willing to destroy myself to remain married to a person who denies I have any needs other than his."

Two years later she wrote to us that she took action to divorce Giorgio: "The price to stay married to him was too huge for me to pay. Giorgio was shocked. He still didn't get it."

## 6. The Unfairness of Clashing Family Values

When couples who love each other discover after marriage that they are miles apart regarding the family values they want to live by in their relationship, charges of unfairness become voiced. For example, Julia comes from a missionary family, and her parents continue to dedicate their lives to serving people less fortunate than themselves. Julia's mother has always been a bundle of energy. Not only does she gladly give 100 percent of herself to help others, she is also a perfectionist who makes sure her house is spotless and always in order. Julia's father is a kind man with firm convictions about not smoking or drinking. His income has always been modest and the family carefully watched every penny spent.

On the other hand, Julia married Dan, who came from a fun-loving, upper-middle-class background. His father was in real estate, and the family never had to worry about how much money they could spend. His father drank excessively at times and smoked cigars. He speculated in buying and selling stocks and was successful at it. Dan's mother, in contrast to Julia's, is self-centered and believes she is a martyr, that no one in her family appreciates her, and she complains no one does enough to satisfy her needs. She makes Dan feel guilty about not visiting her more often, since Dan and Julia live on the West Coast and she lives in the Chicago.

Despite these differences in values (Dan smokes cigars, likes to drink, and has a tendency to overspend and speculate in the stock market, and Julia disapproves of all of these behaviors), they have been able to set their differences aside in the raising of their one child, John, now four. Indeed, they can well be proud of the loving care they have devoted toward raising their child. John shows it in his secure, happy behavior. However, Julia is very angry because she believes Dan doesn't help enough around the house. Dan in turn complains, "I do a lot but it's never enough for Julia. I also stopped smoking in the house and limited my drinking to two glasses of wine a night, but she still complains, with never a thank you for trying. I made a modest investment in a new PC stock issue that doubled my money, and all Julia said was that I was lucky this time but I would lose the next time—and she hoped there wouldn't be a next time."

In reality, John did far more housework than most men, but it was never enough for Julia. Julia was a perfectionist like her mother, and felt guilty because she did not have her mother's drive and energy to match her mother's housekeeping abilities. She also had her mother's tendency to sacrifice herself for the needs of others. Dan complained, "She sends out one hundred fifty Christmas cards with long notes included and exhausts herself doing it. I really am concerned about her health; she vacuums every day and everything is kept spotless, but she's exhausted. I tell her to relax a little. We can afford a part-time housekeeper, but no, Julia feels that would show she's lazy. To me it's just common sense. My family always had a housekeeper."

Another values clash between them is the issue of how many times a year they should visit Dan's family. "Four times a year, at least," Dan says. "One time a year is more than enough," Julia says. Dan feels he's in a double-bind; his mother makes him feel guilty if he doesn't visit her at least four times a year, while Julia says his first obligation is to his own family, Julia and John, and that four times a year is unfair and traumatic in its effect on their child.

Both accuse each other of being selfish and uncaring. However, their differences are derived from the unconscious value-programming each received in their respective families. Julia and Dan are a decent, nonmanipulative, well-intentioned couple who clash because each of them grew up in a different value system. If they chose to focus on the unconscious value-imprinting they received from their parents, they could then dispense with blaming and name-calling and take the steps needed to modify their behavior: Julia to be less the perfectionist and caretaker; Dan to be less the free-wheeling spendthrift and stock market speculator, who also can resist the demands of his mother to see more of him than is convenient for his own family. Their marriage is still at risk, since both of them are still in their I'd-rather-be-right-than-happy mode of behavior; each are still accusing the other of being unfair. In fact, Julia recently got the name and phone number of a divorce lawyer from a friend and is debating with herself whether she should call him.

## 7. The Unfairness of the Policeman Relationship

"I can't even go to the bathroom without Brian getting suspicious," Shannon says. "We've been married four years, and having an affair never entered my mind. Yet Brian always wants me to account for every minute I'm away from him. When I tried to keep a secret that I went shopping for a birthday present for him last week, he blew his top and accused me of every crime in the book—I was unfaithful and deceitful, a manipulative liar, and those were the nicest words he used. And all I wanted to do was surprise him! I know Brian respects my intelligence and career ability and he says he's still crazy over my looks, but he's always trying to control me. If I'm late, even a half-hour, coming home from the office because of a traffic jam, he starts raving that I'm having an affair and not telling him about it. If I visit a girlfriend's home, he calls up to make sure I'm there. When we're at a party, if I talk to a man for more than five minutes he accuses me of starting up an affair. He's such a great guy in so many ways, but he's driving me crazy. When we married I thought I had a partner, not a policeman."

When we looked more deeply into Brian's growing up background, it turned out that his mother had left his father half a dozen times for other men. She always came back, but the tension and mistrust between his parents never ended. Brian always lived in fear that once again his mother might leave him and his father. He had unconsciously generalized his mistrust to all women, particularly his wife. He loved his wife, as indeed he loved his mother, but he transferred his fear that his mother would abandon him to his wife. It was as if at the unconscious level he was still that frightened little boy who loved his mother but mistrusted her because she might disappear. And to make sure she didn't leave him, he felt driven to control her every move. The only difference was that Shannon was not his mother; he had created a fearful fantasy in place of the flesh-and-blood woman who was his wife.

Men often burden themselves with this feeling of fear of ultimate abandonment by the partner they love the most. Belief in equality at the conscious level can clash with punitive inequality at the unconscious level. Unfortunately, Brian continued to "drive Shannon crazy." A year and a half later Shannon filed for divorce.

• • •

## Pseudo-Unfairness

Also prevalent in today's times are marital relationships that "appear" to be unfair, but really are not based on any deliberate or malicious attempts to inject inequality and injustice into a partnership. In these situations, both the husband and wife are victimized by external circumstances they are unaware of. Once these external circumstances are brought to awareness, both husband and wife can join forces to eliminate their divisive effect on their relationship, providing they are able to correct this gross misunderstanding before their conflicts have escalated into a mountain of injustice-collecting by both of them.

The typical external circumstances that give rise to this mislabeling (which we call "pseudo-unfairness") are the consequences of a genetic predisposition to illness that can cause a person to act out harmful behavior toward his (or her) partner without any intent to do so other than a compulsion over which there seems to be no control.

The three most prevalent genetic predispositions toward illnesses that create divisiveness and feelings of unfairness in a relationship are being an adult child of an alcoholic, chronic depression or manic-depression, and adult attention deficit disorder. Following are some examples of how these illnesses can create the false impression that a person is deliberately acting unjustly toward one's partner.

## The Injustice-Collecting Lifestyle of Adult Children of Alcoholics

Diana can't understand why her husband Tim can turn from a loving husband into a raging tiger almost instantly. Whenever he drinks more than two drinks, he becomes an angry man spoiling for a fight and is critical of everything Diana does. And when things don't turn out as he expects them to, he becomes bitterly disappointed. "No matter how trivial the issue is, he acts as if he's been betrayed," Diana says. "For instance, we went to a play the other night anticipating it would be very entertaining because the reviews were good. Well, it was pretty boring instead. No big deal, sometimes you don't win out. But it was a big, big deal for Tim, who grumbled until the next day about how the critics steered him wrong. You would think it was the end of the world. And when I leave him for a day to visit my sick mother who lives in another city, he pouts like a little kid and always makes me feel guilty about going. He's also self-centered and impulsive and can act like I don't exist, like last week when he went out and bought a new TV that caught his fancy. He never bothered to talk to me in advance about it. It's expensive and I saw no need for it. He just impulsively bought it when he was browsing in a department store. It's like that all the time; he's so unfair to me."

Tim couldn't handle drinking because his parents were alcoholics, and he had inherited the family's genetic predisposition to alcoholism. It would be best to eliminate drinking altogether to help him and his marriage. Tim's impulsivity came from his parents being alcoholic: he couldn't count on them to live up to any agreement they would make with him, like saying they would go to his Little League game on Saturday, then forgetting to do so because they would be drunk by then. So Tim learned to impulsively act on what he wanted because he couldn't count on planning ahead since he would always be disappointed. Get what you want while the getting's good, otherwise it will disappear by tomorrow, was the imprinting he received from his parents. It turned out he had been terrified over the frequent times when his parents left him alone and disappeared at an overnight drinking party with their friends.

Tim was causing great harm to his marriage by unconsciously replicating all of these learned behaviors which he could eliminate once he uncovered where they originated. With the compassionate assistance of Diana, he was able to temper his impulsivity, to eliminate drinking entirely by attending the Adult Children of Alcoholics group in his city, to recognize that being disappointed over an unanticipated happening is not a form of parental betrayal, and to understand that when Diana visits her mother, she is not abandoning him like his parents did when they went on a drunken tear.

In this example, there was enough love left in their relationship, and enough personal motivation on Tim's part to go to counseling and eliminate his drinking and change his behavior to improve the marriage. A wife will take divorce action if these elements are lacking in their marriage.

### The Manic-Depressive Injustice

"He becomes vicious; maybe I married a mean person and he just pretended he loved me to get me to marry him." This is Jessica, pouring out her agony over her marriage to Wayne. "He goes through cycles—he has these spurts of energy where he's real fun-loving, happy and excited about life, then suddenly he'll turn and be in the dumps for weeks, and then it's hard for him even to say hello to me. I can forget about lovemaking when he's like that. I never know when he's going to switch from being super-happy to feeling very sad and totally helpless, hopeless, and suicidal. I tell him to get a grip on himself and think happy thoughts when he has the blues, but it's as if he doesn't want to hear me. It's so unfair; I'm always walking on eggshells trying to attend to his needs and getting no acknowledgment from him. Instead, he's so self-centered it's as if he thinks I'm his enemy rather than his wife when I try to snap him out of his blue funks."

What Wayne was suffering from was a classic case of manic-depression, a genetically based disease that was transmitted to him from his father's family where cases of manic-depression were prevalent. Wayne did not know this but thought it was a sign of his lack of character that he couldn't control his cyclical behavior, his highs and lows. Until recently, most men and women experiencing this behavior never knew it was a medical disorder. Recent medical breakthroughs have identified this behavior as a medical disorder rather than a failure of character. This fact has been given wide publicity in the media, along with the encouraging fact that appropriate medication, such as Lithium, can mitigate the effect of manic-depression on one's behavior. Now that Wayne and Jessica know that his disease needs to be managed, they are working together as a team and no longer misread and mislabel the intentions each feels toward the other. Wayne is now taking appropriate medication under the careful guidance of a psychopharmacologist. Their relationship has vastly improved since, in addition to medication, psychological counseling has enabled them to become compassionately understanding of each other. This is a course of action available to the many couples in our society who are experiencing similar difficulties. Hope is on their horizon.

On the other hand, far too many people still believe manic-depression is a sign of personal weakness instead of an illness. When that ignorance persists, a divorce will occur, or the marriage will continue to be experienced as chronic pain and anger over being unfairly treated.

### The Injustice of the Adult Attention Deficit Disorder Spouse

Megan says Quentin, her husband, always seems to be "out to lunch." "Even when I try to talk to him seriously and need his attention, his eyes start to wander; he fidgets in his chair or gets up and walks around the room when I'm talking. I yell at him to listen to me while his back is turned to me and he says, 'Don't yell. Of course I'm hearing you.' He's so rude he can drive me out of my mind. Forgetful—you better believe it. I give him a grocery list and he comes back with items I didn't want because he loses the list. I can't count on him to watch the kids because he'll forget to put them to bed on time or not pay attention when they might be destroying their toys or fighting with each other. I feel I have three kids in my family—my two sons plus my husband."

What Megan thought was that Quentin was just being stubborn and wanted to harm her by deliberately being rude, inattentive, and forgetful. This was not the case at all, because Quentin was suffering without knowing it from Adult Attention Deficit Disorder. This is a recently discovered disorder that is genetically based. It was previously thought that only hyperactive children could have an Attention Deficit Disorder. New medical findings have demonstrated that children with this disorder, known as ADD, can continue to carry this disorder into adulthood. It was once thought ADD disappeared in adulthood. But it is now known that at least ten million adults continue to live with this disorder. Adults with ADD are prone to distractions: They get bored very quickly; they cannot maintain consistent behavior; they are forgetful and find it almost impossible to plan ahead since they are forever impulsive. All of these characteristics were evidenced in Quentin's behavior, which Megan misread as his being deliberately and maliciously unfair to her.

Both Megan and Quentin learned too late that Quentin had a genetically based disorder that could be managed and modified through the use of appropriate medication like Ritalin and antidepressant drugs combined with psychological counseling. Sixteen years of misreading and misinterpreting each other had taken its toll on both of them. Megan divorced Quentin, and it was three years after their divorce that she and Quentin found out the real cause of Quentin's aberrant behavior. By then neither of them wished to try to renew their relationship because they could not eliminate their bitterness toward each other.

• • •

## How Women View Unfairness

I believe that most men have the best of intentions, and really want to treat women fairly, but frankly they don't understand how women feel about unfairness. I asked Pat about this dilemma, and here is what she suggested for divorced women who are starting to date again.

I've heard many women give up trying to change their husband's behavior and express their hopelessness to me. However, there is a way out of their dilemma. Men can be educated to understand why women feel unfairly treated, and they can correct their behavior because they also believe in fairness.

I'm concerned about how inappropriately most women respond to unfair treatment by men. On the one hand, many women demonize all men after their divorce, and then react to each new man they date as if he were this stereotype instead of a well-intentioned person, who should be alerted in a nonthreatening way to the unfair condition he may be creating out of his unawareness so that it may be corrected.

Many women try to model themselves after men because they think that's the way to succeed in business and the world. They remember their male bosses who were aggressive. They remember these bosses succeeded at the expense of other people, and as a result of seeing this at work, they may develop an aggressive mannerism. Women today have few role models they can look up to as successful women who have what I believe is our special female quality of connecting with people rather than stomping on them. The trouble is this "tough" male aggressive attitude has led men into disaster in the field of interpersonal family relationships, and women who are also aggressive are discovering it's also leading them to a dead end.

On the other hand, there are many unassertive women of all ages in our society. You would think that since we are living in a time of rising expectations for women's roles in society, unassertiveness would be a thing of the past. But that simply isn't so. It's naïve to believe you can wipe out the imprinting you received growing up in your family overnight—or just because you say you want it to disappear. Most of these unassertive women want to be assertive, but they just can't muster it up because they were born into families—remember, that was in the '50s—where they imitated their mother's behavior. They learned from their mothers that women must be submissive, be the caretaker, tend to household duties, and never make waves. They were told never to take the last piece of cake.

Significant traces of these old attitudes still exist now that they have grown up. Their mothers told them to get a career along with getting married, but they didn't educate them to become assertive too. It was a mixed message. So it isn't surprising that many women stifle their resentment against what they believe is their husband's unfair treatment of them. They are afraid to be assertive and confuse assertiveness with aggression and being "unfeminine."

That, of course, is absurd. To be assertive is neither masculine or feminine. It is simply the appropriate way to act to get your needs met. To be assertive is an expression of your own self-esteem. It doesn't attack another person because assertiveness is framed in the context of I-statements rather than accusatory You-statements. It's an expression of "I need," or "I am concerned," or "I'd like to draw your attention to what is making me uncomfortable," rather than the aggressive act of stating "You are hurting me," or "You are always insensitive," or "You always . . ." Aggression causes people to be defensive and become counteraggressive, while being assertive gets the attention of a partner in a nonthreatening way, which enables problems to be solved rather than intensified.

Since so few role models for women exist in society today that meet the needs of these demanding times, it's incumbent upon women to become their own role model. Heading the list of components that are required for today's new woman role model is the need to practice true assertiveness in all relationships. Never hold back or stifle your feelings, for doing so will eventually tear up a relationship. Timing is important, so bring up your concerns at an appropriate time. To be assertive is to build up your sense of self-esteem, which is an essential requirement for eliminating injustice-collecting in your relationship.

• • •

## How Men View Unfairness

I asked Mel how men viewed unfairness in marriage relationships. Here is what he said:

Men haven't a clue as to the depths of women's feelings about the need to remedy what they perceive to be unfairness in their marriages. I can speak for myself on this issue. It took me many years to understand why women feel that, in general, they have been unfairly treated, not only in marriage but in divorce and in society at large.

I have two grown-up daughters, and they have taught me much about the world as women view it. It's still a man's world, they say. Women are unfairly treated in the working world, earning only seventy-five cents where men earn a dollar for equivalent work. There is a glass ceiling in business where the top management jobs in 95 percent of the cases still go to men. And when both husband and wife work the same hours each week, it's the wife who spends twice as much time as her husband in cooking, cleaning, shopping, and tending to the children's needs. Women believe there is lots of hypocrisy in the claim that men and women are now justly treated as equals in society and married life.

When my daughters shared these observations with me, they did so with an undercurrent of deep emotion that emphasized how these facts affect their own experiences in life. On the other hand, we men believe the world we grew up in, where men are considered the major power-wielders and decision-makers, is both natural, normal, and fair—that role is attached to us from birth.

A recent female client, Melissa, made me sharply aware of the difference between men and women in their views of society. Melissa is thirty-five and is still angry at how society treats women. She told me that as a child she used to stuff Kleenex down in front of her genitals to give the impression she had a penis. No, it wasn't penis envy, she said. It was male privileges envy, since she saw her two brothers receiving favored treatment and a far wider latitude of freedom than she received, simply because they were boys.

More often than not, women's grievances against male insensitivity and the male desire to always rule the roost are justified. But male-bashing isn't going to solve the problem. Men and women need one another—that's the glory of life—and all four-letter words and putdowns of men do is tear the sexes even further apart. Despite all the hype about men and women coming from different planets, we really come from the *same* planet. We're in this life together, and the bottom line is that men and women want the same thing: love and caring friendship from each other. Men really have the best intentions toward women—all surveys show, for example, that men think it's only fair that women should be paid the same as men for equal work. Men will respond to fairness if women will educate them, not hit them over the head with a baseball bat, as to the kinds of behavior they identify as unfairness.

I can remember Pat telling me it was unfair that she not only prepared all our meals but did the dishes too. She worked equally as hard as I did, but also undertook the entire burden of cooking and cleaning up after meals while I looked at the TV news. Until it was brought to my attention, I didn't know it was "unfair" because I grew up in a household where my mother did everything, since as a boy I was favored over my sister. But today is another world, and women acutely perceive the injustice of old family behavior. I had believed my nonparticipation in doing the dishes was "normal," not unfair, until Pat brought it to my attention. Yes, I changed. I now do the dishes because it's the right thing to do. I don't particularly like to do them, but it's only fair, so I do them.

I don't think I'm any different from any other man. We will respond to requests for fairness from the wife we love when we are educated by her as to what she considers unfair. The problem often gets compounded by women's failure to communicate appropriately what they perceive to be unfair. They may express dissatisfaction through verbal attacks, blame-making, and name-calling. But on the other hand, they may not express anything at all. Instead they will simmer with resentment inside themselves, waiting for the husband to get the message. "If he really cares for me, he'll know how unfair he is and correct his behavior without my telling him," is the attitude that underpins her silence as she suffers with what she considers the unfair behavior of her spouse. On the other hand, her spouse, not being a mindreader, thinks everything is going famously well in their relationship because he hears no overt complaint from his wife. Both of them are on a collision course, unaware that they are creating it.

It's time to put an end to the absurd notion that men and women can't compassionately understand each other. Educating each other kindly in a spirit of goodwill as to the justice of their needs is the medicine that can cure their differences.

• • •

## How Divorce Can Become the Ultimate Form of Injustice-Collecting

For those men and women who love injustice-collecting more than they love each other, divorce becomes the arena after their marriage ends in which new injustices can be found. It's easy for them to do so, for the new injustices are of their own making. There is the classic case we observed of a couple who fought legal battles for three years over who should get custody of their upright piano. The wife eventually "won" the case. The legal costs amounted to sixty-five thousand dollars, but the piano itself was worth only six hundred dollars! And neither the former husband nor wife could play the piano! (The piano had been a wedding gift twenty years ago that had become a fixture in their living room.)

In their divorce, the only thing they were playing was "getting even," rather than the piano. Since each knew the other wanted the piano in the divorce settlement, neither of them was going to allow that to happen under any circumstances. Each viewed their divorce as pay back time for all the injustices they believed they had experienced in their marriage. "Winning" the piano, therefore, would prove the winner was right and the ex-spouse wrong about who was the alleged evil-doer that caused the marriage to become a nightmare.

Of course, all this rationalization was a fevered fantasy burning out of control in each of their minds. For the only "winners" in this court case were their lawyers, who happily banked the giant fees that the modest piano generated. The couple needed to learn that trying to "get even" with their former spouse by hurling accusations of unfair treatment at each other like poisoned darts and trying to prevent an equal distribution of property and income accumulated during their marriage as a form of punishment is a no-win game. Both became losers, since no matter how much they "won" from the other in a court battle, it would never be enough to assuage the pain of their shattered marriage.

Injustice-collectors of this type are really trying to compare apples with oranges: on the one hand, there is the traumatic pain involved in the loss of what were the most valuable things in one's life—a loving relationship and the dream of a shared happy life together that would last a lifetime; on the other hand, there is the painful loss of income and material goods that is an initial inevitable consequence of divorce (what two once owned together must now be split separately). The fair thing to do is to accept that fact of life as reality, rather than an affliction from God or your ex-spouse, and then reach a settlement based on the fact that a wife was an equal partner in the marriage and deserves an equal share of the economic wealth accumulated during the life of that marriage. After that, you are free to concentrate on the constructive new opportunities that await you in your single state.

The piano obsessed couple—Hal and Dora were their names—had trapped themselves into believing that the pain in the "apple" of their past marriage could be remedied by the "orange" of winning a court case against one's partner. But all they could do was win something material. The spiritual loss of their marriage was lost forever. No amount of material wealth could compensate for that loss. Ironically, Hal and Dora had "paid" already for the loss of their marriage while they were still married. They had paid for it in the pain they had inflicted on each other in the bitter fights they had over Hal's excessive drinking, in the betrayal of trust resulting from affairs both had when they felt rejected by their spouse, in the dislike they had of each other's friends, in the battles over sex denied or found unsatisfying, in the verbal abuse used to knife-wound each other—words like "bitch," "bastard," and "fuck you"—that ended almost every argument. Their divorce offered them the opportunity to end the getting-even game, but they refused to take it.

We heard about Hal and Dora recently. It's ten years later now, and Hal is on his third divorce and complaining once more about how his wife is ripping him off, just like his other two did. And Dora has decided that all men are bastards and leads a solitary life with her two cats. Both Hal and Dora remain trapped in their past. For them, the present is not an opportunity but a disaster bound to happen just around the corner.

For the many marriage and divorce injustice-collectors in this world, any irrelevant item or issue can be transformed into an injustice. If an ex-wife wants the record collection, the ex-husband will be sure to create a court fight over who gains its possession. A mountain bike, a chair, a table, a dog, a cat, a parrot, an umbrella—you name it and by lighting the fire of righteous indignation it becomes worth fighting over if the ex-spouse wants it!

These tortured, love-turned-to-hate relationships that are acted out in a divorce can continue long after a legal divorce has occurred. It's as if the divorce has never really ended their marriage. This can and does inhibit such injustice-collectors from taking advantage of the opportunity to experience a creative divorce in which the past is laid to rest to make way for a better future. This phenomenon is so widespread we are devoting the next entire chapter to its consideration.

# 6

# WHEN DIVORCE BECOMES THE MARRIAGE THAT NEVER ENDS

When we compare divorce today to the time when Pat and I were divorced in the 1970s, it seems everything has changed: divorce today is acknowledged as an ongoing fact in American life rather than as a dirty little secret; divorce counseling is an extensive profession instead of being nonexistent; discussions about divorce are TV and radio talk show staples; resources for the divorced are available from religious organizations as well as social work agencies; there are even divorce announcements designed to look like marriage announcements. . . .

Yet the more things change, the more they remain the same. I saw an example of this fact the other day. I was having lunch with my friend Len, who was divorced two years ago and had just begun to date again. The first three women he dated turned out to be disasters. He said, "When I asked them whether or not they were divorced, I expected them to acknowledge in a sentence or two what their status was and then go on from there to find out more about them as individuals. Instead, what I had done without knowing it was to open the floodgates to tirades about what bastards their ex-husbands were, how they were screwed in their divorce settlements, and how their ex-husbands were always behind in their support payments.

"One of them—her name was Judy—really blew my mind. After listening to her rant and rave against her ex-husband, I asked her how long she had been divorced. She looked surprised, as if it was the most irrelevant question in the world, and said she had been divorced twelve years ago! She even said, 'Why do you ask?' It was like she had never been divorced. She was still carrying her ex with her wherever she went, being so damned righteous about herself."

Len then asked me, "Is this what I'm always going to be faced with when I date?" I told him not to be discouraged. It is true that there are all too many women, and men too, who act like the women Len talked about. In fact, it is such a prevalent phenomenon that it seems like an inevitable consequence of divorce. However, this is a false conclusion since so very many women and men use divorce as a stepping-stone to improving the quality of their present lives, rather than seeing themselves as victims helplessly mired in the past. Len will be able to meet such people as he continues to socialize more frequently.

Ironically, divorced women and men who complain throughout the years about their past marriages and the "wickedness" and "rottenness" of their ex-spouses perpetuate the bitter marital feelings that their legal divorce was supposed to end. Consequently, for these women and men, divorce becomes the continuation of their past marriage by other means and can embitter them to their dying day.

Why should fundamentally intelligent and decent people act in such a self-defeating way that alienates them from the men and women they would like to attract? Why do they remain trapped in agonizing over past hurts and injustices? Their past has become their present.

Separating the past from the present is essential if you are to have a creative divorce. Otherwise you will continue to have a Marriage That Never Ends instead of an *emotional* as well as legal divorce that frees you to improve upon your past life rather than trap yourself in it.

Pat and I have helped many such women and men move from living in a bitter past to a brighter present for themselves. Following are the suggestions that helped them do so.

• • •

## The Nine Ways to Divorce Yourself from the Marriage That Never Ends

### 1. Understand that fear is what keeps you chained to the Marriage That Never Ends.

To experience divorce is to experience fear—the fear that you may not be able to make it on your own now that you are no longer part of a couple. Since divorce is the second-most traumatic experience in a person's life (remember, next to the death of a loved one, divorce ranks as the most emotionally devastating experience one can live through), the fear of not making it on one's own is universal in the initial stage of divorce. However, by taking personal responsibility to successfully respond to the challenges and opportunities that exist in the present, divorced persons usually can overcome their fear within the first years of their divorce. They then successfully get on with their new single-person life, so that savaging their ex-spouse becomes irrelevant and unnecessary. The excitement of living well in the present transcends the need to focus on past bitterness and regrets in order to give meaning to their daily lives.

When a divorced person feels his or her present life is in disarray, with the future appearing as a huge question mark, the tendency will be to seek comfort in the past, even if that past has been bitter, miserable, and hurtful. The comfort of familiar past pain, under this circumstance, is unconsciously preferred to seeing oneself as a person who doesn't have the resources to cope successfully with the present problems in his or her life, such as finding a good career with decent pay, coping with children as a "single" parent, or obtaining a new love relationship that improves upon the past rather than repeats it.

Therefore, complaining that all of your present problems are your ex-spouse's fault becomes the comforting cop-out that masks the fear that you may be incapable of solving your problems on your own. The longer your present life is out of control because you don't take personal responsibility to make positive things happen to you, the longer you will continue to perpetuate your past marriage *in your feelings* through bad-mouthing your ex-spouse.

Flash forward and you will find many persons like Judy answering the question, "How long have you been divorced?" with the reply, "Twenty-two years, of course!" Instead of creating a fulfilling life for themselves, they have made a lifetime occupation out of regurgitating the bitterness of their past marriage.

## 2. Break the I'd-rather-be-right-than-happy addiction.

Why is the bitterness and bad-mouthing of one's ex so hard to give up even when good friends draw attention to the fact that no positive purpose is served by playing the old see-what-that-rat-has-done-to-me record over and over and over again?

The reason why this broken record continues to be replayed despite the fact that it changes nothing for the better, and instead intensifies the helplessness of the person playing that record, is that the person has become addicted to the I'd-rather-be-right-than-happy fix.

If your sense of self-esteem is low, if you feel powerless, if you feel you are the person to whom things happen rather than the person who makes things happen, then you'll derive a false sense of power by taking a daily I'd-rather-be-right-than-happy fix. As a result, you create a new career for yourself, one of "proving" all your problems are due to your divorce and that wretch of an ex who is forever plaguing your life. It's a career that can last a lifetime, because spending a lifetime proving you are "right" and that your ex is a towering evil monster hides the fear that you can't take effective charge of your life in the present. Instead, the I'd-rather-be-right-than-happy fix provides you with:

*False Comfort in Being the Victim.*

"Poor me," says Carol. "Dylan left me without a cent three years ago and I'm almost thirty; no career, no nothing. The best of my life is already over and nobody will ever love me again. It's all the fault of that bastard."

*False Power in "Getting Even" and in Revenge Fantasies.*

Jennifer, who is thirty-five and has two daughters, seven and five, passionately dedicates her life to fantasizing the murder of Ron, her ex-husband whom she divorced four years ago. "I learned later he had many more than the one affair I knew about when I divorced him. That rat! I still dream that maybe he'll crash in the next plane he flies, or that he'll be mugged. I'll be damned if I'll let him see my kids as often as he wants to!"

*False Security in Self-Righteousness.*

Michelle, now thirty-four, knows she did everything right in her marriage to Brian, which ended three years ago. "I was the perfect housewife and did everything to make Brian happy. He had nothing to complain about, so I was shocked when he said he wanted the divorce. It only proves no man can be trusted. They're all after only one thing and don't have any feelings at all. Even so, I'd like to get married again, but most of my dates never call again."

*The Person-Left-Behind Divorce: Forever Angry.*

Feeling bitter and angry and helpless, the person left behind, shocked because his or her partner wanted out of the marriage, may play the victim role for the rest of his or her life. It becomes harder and harder to risk the new and easier to wallow in helplessness.

*The Person-Who-Leaves Divorce: Forever Self-Righteous.*

Believing all the misery in the marriage is the fault of "that turkey I married," the person leaves. But only to find out that new problems are created once the separation begins: the single scene out there is not that great, sex is scary, and the economics of divorce are a nightmare. With this disillusionment, resulting from unrealistic expectations, a sense of victimization equally as virulent as the feelings of the person left behind can occur. Carefully nurtured, that sense of victimization can also last a lifetime. The excuse being: "If my spouse had been a better person, I wouldn't have had to leave and be in the mess I'm now in."

*The Let's-Continue-to-Be-Friends Divorce.*

The image of two nice people having a "friendly" divorce starts to crack when arguments over who gets what in the divorce settlement begin to occur. The "friendliness" is found out to be the cover for deep-seated resentments over the breakup of the marriage. Feelings of betrayal can predominate and the temptation to use the I'd-rather-be-right-than-happy fix may be too great to avoid.

Jessica, a forty-five-year-old friend of Pat's, was finally able to divorce herself from her own Marriage That Never Ended. She told Pat:

"I learned the hard way that always complaining about the way my ex-husband treated me whenever I went out may have alienated my dates," she said. "I kept wondering why a nice woman like me, bright and attractive, spent so many Saturday nights alone. Then it dawned on me that perhaps I might be someone men would avoid. I wasn't showing my attractiveness to the new men I was dating. Instead, I was showing them the bitterness of an unhappy and angry woman. No man likes to hear you attacking another man. He feels uncomfortable when you do that and thinks: 'Well, she must really believe all men are rotten, so maybe I'll be the next guy she'll attack'. It's no surprise that I probably was seen as a fatal disease to be avoided rather than the woman I am, who enjoys the company of men. So when I realized I was shooting myself with my mouth, I took away the gun."

Pat said that two years later she received a wedding invitation from Jessica. The man she married was one she met after she stopped bad-mouthing her ex. Her personal note on the card read, "Living well is the best revenge!"

That, indeed, is how you break the I'd-rather-be-right-than-happy addiction—by focusing on making yourself happy in the present rather than broadcasting your rage against your ex to every new person you date. Continue reading to learn how to arrive at this goal.

## 3. Remember the words of W.C. Fields and apply them to your situation.

The great comedian, W. C. Fields, offered the following good advice: "If at first you don't succeed, try, try again. Then stop. Stop making a fool of yourself." Notice if there is a pattern to your behavior. Do you repeatedly talk negatively about your ex-spouse on every new date? Do you still continue to have revenge fantasies about him or her even though it's been years since your divorce? Does the hope for a good new love relationship begin to seem like an impossible dream? Then it's time to acknowledge that you may be creating your own problems and take personal responsibility to change your behavior.

## 4. Recognize that you may be stuck in the first stage of the mourning process of divorce (the "Why Me?" Stage) long after it is appropriate.

Mourning the death of your marriage is necessary if you are to let go of the past and begin to renew your life in a positive way as a single person. In the "Why Me?" Stage, feelings of anger, revenge, and being a victim predominate. The marriage is still very much alive in your feelings, even though you may have a legal piece of paper that says you are divorced. Letting go of your marriage requires you to move from the "Why Me?" Stage of the mourning process to the "Letting Go" and "Self-Renewal"

Stages, in which you no longer need to be angry and revenge-obsessed against your ex-spouse since you feel secure and confident that you can create your own happiness as a single person.

### 5. Seek out a good professional divorce counselor to assist you in getting unstuck from the first stage of the mourning process.

It is not a sign of personal failure to acknowledge you are too close to your situation to deal skillfully with it. In fact, it is the strong person who recognizes the need for professional help when he or she is too close to the problem to see it clearly.

### 6. View your past marriage as a learning experience rather than a disaster inflicted upon you by your ex.

Most people who use their divorce as a stepping-stone for their self-renewal learn that there were no villains or evil-doers in their breakup. Instead, there were two well-meaning people who created a collision-course relationship with each other out of unawareness of what they were doing: they didn't treat each other as equals; they exhibited little empathy toward each other; they spent little time nourishing their relationship; they intensified resentments toward each other instead of resolving arguments. They learned it takes two to make a relationship turn sour, so they took personal responsibility to make sure their own self-defeating behaviors that existed in their marriage would be eliminated from their new relationships. You, too, can learn what they have learned.

### 7. Understand that your anger is fear-based, and that you have nothing to fear but fear itself.

Your anger is telling you more about yourself than about your ex-spouse. By ascribing the source of your present unhappiness to your past resentments against your ex, you may be hiding the fear that you cannot make positive things happen in your life as a single person. Indeed, positive things won't happen in your life when you become permanently attached to your past marriage by continuing to fan the flames of your anger against your ex. Letting go of that anger enables you to lead a richer present life, since you have underestimated your capacity not only to survive as a single person, but also to triumph over the challenges that single life presents.

### 8. Eliminate black-hat versus white-hat thinking from your mind.

Blame-making is nourished when you always see yourself as wearing the white hat, always being in the right, and seeing your ex in the black hat, always being in the wrong. This serves no useful purpose, since blame-making is flame-making; it stokes the fires of self-righteousness within you. However, it doesn't make you any happier. It's like a mosquito bite that you scratch: while you're scratching you might feel better, but once you stop, you are left feeling worse than if you hadn't scratched.

## 9. Practice forgiveness in place of revenge.

The next time you start to generate a revenge fantasy against your ex, ask yourself what purpose does it serve? How does it help you? Does it enable you to become a more loving, a more caring person, or does it simply add another embittered wrinkle around your mouth?

Revenge fantasies and actions initiated in revenge are wasted uses of the energy you possess, which could be freed by you to improve the quality of your life if you would permit it to happen. Revenge drags you back into an injustice-collecting past.

Sheldon Kopp has stated that "Revenge is a form of nostalgia." It is a yearning for a past that never was, one that you imagine might have been perfect if it wasn't for that monster who was your ex. But will "paying him (or her) back" or "getting even" remake that past? Will you be any happier if the fantasy of his or her falling off a cliff became a reality?

Instead, substitute forgiveness for revenge, and positive things will begin to happen in your life. When you come to the realization that both you and your ex-spouse married because you loved each other, with the intent it would be for life, that you did harmful things to each other, not because either of you was a wicked person but because you acted unskillfully in solving your marital problems, that you meant to do the best for each other, although it often turned out otherwise—then you can forsake revenge and forgive your ex (and yourself) and get on with the necessary business of your life. That business is living well, which indeed is the best form of "revenge."

# 7

# PARENTS ARE FOREVER: MAINTAINING HEALTHY RELATIONSHIPS WITH YOUR CHILDREN

For men and women with children of *any* age, divorce becomes a challenge to maintain or establish or re-establish caring and loving relationships with them, no matter how alienated you are from each other. How well you will relate to your children in the years ahead, and how they will relate to you, is critically dependent on the way you handle your separation and legal divorce.

Think for a moment about what "the divorce made in hell" does to the self-esteem and love children feel towards themselves and their parents. When parents perpetuate the injustice-collecting war against each other that began in their marriage and continues in unabated fury in their separation and divorce, it can have a devastatingly negative effect on their children's social and psychological well-being.

When children hear their parents repeatedly call each other "bitch," "bastard," "deadbeat," "untrustworthy," "manipulative," "worthless," "cruel," or "irresponsible" in the heat of their divorce—and maintain these attitudes long after the end of the marriage—the children learn to mistrust themselves and the world. Parents are the children's entire world in the early years of their development. Even with all the talk about social and economic factors causing so much insecurity, anxiety, anger, envy, and bitterness in children these days, parents are the primary determinants of their children's outlook, behavior, and ability to cope constructively with the slings and arrows of this world. This does not mean that economic and social factors are irrelevant. To the contrary, it is extremely important to have support systems such as decent schools, a crime-free, drug-free community, and decent jobs at decent pay. But parents come first. They are the ground children learn to stand on, while the support systems are superstructures that can have little or no positive effect if parents themselves don't take primary responsibility in enabling their children to grow up as valued human beings.

Consequently, a child watching his or her parents savaging each other in the divorce learns that the world is a treacherous ocean in which he/she might drown at any time. If you can't count on the persons you love and trust the most—your mother and father who are your entire world in your formative years—who can you count on to give you the security you need when your parents are so insecure themselves?

One bright nine-year-old, Jason, who was experiencing the effects of the divorce-made-in-hell his parents were going through, said to us: "My mom and dad are always fighting, and when I come back from my dad's house, my mom always asks who else was there. If I tell her my dad has a girlfriend, she gets angry and curses him. And my dad does the same when I go to his place. If my mom has a man over, my dad starts to call her bad names. But I love both my mom and dad and I'm scared they don't love me."

What Jason was experiencing, unfortunately, happens to too many children, whether they are in married or divorced households. When parents themselves are insecure and filled with fear, anxiety, and hatred, their children feel their entire world is threatened. Newly divorced parents, in particular, are so fearful and insecure initially about their own survival that they tend to have tunnel vision, focusing primarily on themselves and neglecting the emotional nurturing their children need at this traumatic time in their lives. And if these parents continue to focus on blame-making and injustice-collecting against each other long after their legal divorce takes place, the self-esteem of their children plummets. Translated into adult terms, such children begin to feel: "I am made from both my mom and dad and I love them both. But if my mom thinks my dad is bad, then the half of me that comes from my dad must also be bad. And if my dad thinks my mom is bad, then the other half of me from my mom must also be bad. Does that mean I'm not really worth anything as a person?"

If a boy or girl expressed themselves in the above way to both of their parents, their mother and father would be equally shocked. "Don't my children know I love them very much?" they would say (and have said to us in counseling sessions). "All I'm trying to do is survive, and it's for their sake," they will add.

We tell such parents that it's true that they love their children and deeply care about their welfare, but they are not skillfully communicating that fact by their actions. They need to pay attention to nurturing the emotional security of their children along with focusing on their own adult problems. Without their knowing it, these parents are creating low self-esteem in their own children. This, in turn, could cause endless future antisocial problems, for if children internalize a belief that they are "worthless" or "bad," they tend to confirm that self-criticism in their actions. In effect, they tell themselves, "If I'm bad and can't trust Mom and Dad, then I'll really prove it by stealing, by irresponsible sexual actions, by drug abuse, by defiance of any authority figures, Mom and Dad included."

Since children's parents are their entire world in their formative years and they are totally dependent on them, children tend to believe the world centers on themselves. For example, children have the illusion of being the all-powerful determiners of family life and decisions precisely because they are so vulnerable. They tend to create a fantasy world in which they convince themselves they are the cause of their parents' divorce. How many times have we heard the following "If only" statements from children of divorced parents in counseling sessions:

"If only I ate everything, including my spinach, the night Dad left, he would have stayed."

"If only my report card had all As and Bs, my parents would have stayed together."

"If only I hadn't stolen that bubble gum from the grocery store, there wouldn't be a divorce."

"If only I hadn't refused to do the dishes like I was supposed to, all this divorce would never have happened."

This is just a tiny sample of the endless numbers of "If only's" we have heard from children. They are really cries of pain, wishing they could establish the security in their lives that they have lost. Because of their dependence on adults, they do not care if Mom and Dad are divorced because their parents say they don't love each other. All they worry about is their own security—can their Mom and Dad provide it for them now that Mom lives in one place and Dad another?

Since children are enormously resilient, parents can correct these children's misconceptions of the impact of divorce. However, in order to provide a new, ongoing sense of positive self-esteem in their children and a new stable sense of emotional and physical security, parents need guidelines as to how they can make this come about. It is the objective of this chapter to indicate how you can utilize your divorce to create better relationships with your children and improve the quality of your life together. Since *love*, as we have said, is an action word, your love for your children will manifest itself in the ways you become positive role models they can count on. You can approach divorce as a challenge to *improve* the relationship you had with them when married, rather than believing only disaster lies ahead. The belief that divorce "inevitably" harms children for life is nonsense! It's a product of the brainwashing we receive from the media based on alleged "expert scientific" studies. Such studies are neither "expert" nor "scientific," but purely biased opinions by alleged authorities with axes to grind.

By becoming aware of how children may think and feel about divorce, you can empower yourself to correct their attitudes and behaviors and reassure your children that they did nothing whatsoever to cause your divorce. You can assure them that you love them and that they have nothing to fear, as evidenced by your ability to solve new problems constructively. Above all, you can learn to act in a manner that will allow the children to love *both* parents, even if you no longer love your ex-spouse.

In order to make this happen, we first must eliminate from our consciousness the brainwashing the media and society in general impose on us to make us believe we are "bad" parents because we are divorced.

• • •

## Arm Yourself Against Guilt-Inducing Terminology

When you read newspaper articles or books, or listen to radio or TV reports on divorce, notice carefully the words the media use concerning divorce:

*Broken home* is the term used for a divorced family,
*Single parent* for a parent who has child custody,
*Custodial rights* for a parenting mother or father,
*Absent father* for a noncustodial father,
*Deadbeat fathers* for nonpayment of child support, and
*Visitation rights* for noncustodial parents.

Unfortunately, all of these words are repeated so often that we begin to take them for granted as describing divorces where children are involved. But that is like getting used to breathing polluted air each day and believing it's normal for air to be polluted.

It's a small wonder that many divorced parents who dearly love their children carry a knapsack of unnecessary guilt with them wherever they go. Not that I was any different in my own divorce. It was only when I started to question the conventional wisdom of these phrases (all of which imply divorce is bad, and marriage is good, without making the distinction between good and bad marriages and good and bad divorces) that they ceased to have a hold over me.

It may be impossible to totally do away with these negative phrases, but we can at least change them into something more constructive in our own minds as a way to help ourselves have a creative divorce grounded in fair treatment rather than angry or vengeful feelings.

Let's analyze these "polluted" words, and look at some suggestions for more constructive substitutes:

*Broken Home.*

When you break something, the dictionary states, you have "rendered something unusable." So a broken home is deficient by definition. This term gives the impression that divorce inevitably means permanent damage has been done. The implication is that a couple does a "bad" thing by getting divorced because children now live in a "broken" home.

Instead of "broken home," substitute the phrase "reconfigured home." "Broken home" gives the impression that the old marriage was working well, when it probably wasn't. When a divorce occurs, a *new* family arrangement takes place. Not a broken one.

To "reconfigure" is to rearrange the parts of a relationship. When a child lives in a "reconfigured" home rather than a "broken" home it means he/she has the advantage of living in two places and can have equal access to both the mother and father. Home life is rearranged, not destroyed.

A divorce, by definition, means a married couple can no longer live together but now must go their separate ways. But that does not mean that they must go their separate ways at the expense of their children. They can divorce each other but never their children if they love them.

*Single Parent.*

This ordinarily implies that a mother has custody and that the father is therefore irrelevant. The implication is that dads don't count, almost like it's been a virgin birth. Dads do count, so let's eliminate the phrase "single parent" since it demeans the relationship between a father and his children. A phrase like "co-parenting relationship" may be a good substitute.

*Custodial Rights.*

This implies a parent is little more than a janitor! That's the ordinary definition of a custodian. And the dictionary defines "custody" as "the state of being detained or held under guard, especially by the police." Surely this is not the way we perceive our roles as parents or our view of our children. But like polluted air, the media brainwashes us into accepting this phrase as a "normal" aspect of the divorce process.

Parents are not janitors, nor are children pawns that need to be placed under arrest. Pat and I suggest that substituting the words "parenting rights" would take away the bitter taste that "custodial rights" exhibits. "Parenting rights" implies that two equal adults have a fair and equal chance to act in the best interests of their children so that the children can enjoy the positive benefit of *both* parents in their upbringing.

*Absent Father.*

This phrase gives the impression that once a divorce occurs, the father disappears. The implication is that the mother is the only parent concerned about the children's welfare and that the father doesn't give a damn. Nothing could be farther from the truth. But "absent father" is repeated so often it's bound to create unnecessary guilt in fathers who are divorced from their former spouse, but not from their children.

The phrase borders on slander. "Hell, I'm not 'absent'; I'm very much involved in my two kids' lives," Gene, a divorced man of 40, told us. Here, again, a change to a phrase like "co-parenting relationship" could be an excellent substitute.

*Deadbeat Fathers.*

The implication here is that only fathers can be "deadbeats" when it comes to financial problems. And well-intentioned fathers who wish they could continue child support payments but are unemployed or otherwise unable to pay are lumped together with parents who maliciously refuse to pay child support. "Deadbeat" is too often used as a cuss-word rather than a reality check.

And why not "deadbeat mothers," since they also exist? Better yet, eliminate the phrase entirely. The overwhelming number of fathers who fall behind in support payments do not do so deliberately. They may want to pay, but forces of circumstance can prevent this from happening. With so much downsizing in industry, along with the elimination of jobs when companies move work to countries where labor is cheap, money may be in short supply.

Where men and women work out their divorce problems in the best interest of their children, delayed payments for legitimate reasons may be accepted as a temporary necessity, rather than as a deliberate attempt to punish their ex-spouse, as well as punishing their children. If the term must be used, use "deadbeat *parents*" rather than fathers, since women are as capable as men of inflicting this kind of injury when they are injustice-collectors. As we noted, why not eliminate the phrase entirely, since it is often applied unfairly.

*Visitation Rights.*

A parent who does not have custody or has joint custody is *not* a visitor, but that is the implication of the word "visitation." It is usually applied to divorced men, implying that with regard to their children they are second-class citizens, rather than an equal parent.

When we asked one of our male clients how he felt about having visitation rights, he told us the words felt like someone was sticking a thumb in his eye. "Hell," he said, "I'm no visitor; I see my children as often as my ex does. When the three of them are with me, we're a family and they see me as their father, not as a visitor." We suggest using the phrase "redesigned family rights" in place of "visitation rights."

Children can then understand that both places in which they now live are of equal importance and that their father is not a visitor in their life but the loving father he always was and will continue to be. "Redesign" implies a new arrangement rather than just the elimination of the old one.

Of course, changes in terminology are not the answer to the manyfold problems divorced parents must contend with. But they are indeed helpful in forcing us to rethink our situation in a more positive light and move us toward better relationships with our children.

Nothing is less true than the cliché, "Sticks and stones may break my bones, but words will never hurt me." Words *can* hurt and destroy. That's exactly what happens in most marriages that end in divorce: harsh, bitter, angry, four-letter words and the shouting and rage that accompanies them, are major contributors to the loss of love which tears a relationship apart.

• • •

## How Children View Their World

The children of divorced couples and the children of still-married parents are both exposed to the same cultural, economic, and social climate. They derive their values, outlook, and behavior not only from their parents but also from the outside world. Parents tend to excessively worry about the negative impact their divorce may have on their children, when many problems their children may be experiencing are the consequence of the disquieting society they (and their parents) live in. Those problems need to be addressed in their own right, not as divorce-related issues. Listen to the sobering words of one of these children:

"I'm scared of being killed. I want to live my life to the fullest and do everything. I don't want to be dead."

This is a remark any adult could make. But this isn't an adult speaking: it is Janelle, a ten-year-old voicing her concerns in a recent national KidsPeace poll of children ages ten through thirteen. The two top worries of these children are: "Getting AIDS" (54 percent) and "Dying" (51 percent). "Getting kidnapped" is third (50 percent) and "Using drugs" is fourth (41 percent). KidsPeace spokesman Mark Stubis summarized the results of this poll: "The kids are really scared and confused out there." At a time in their lives when children used to eagerly look forward to becoming adults with exciting lives, half of these youngsters polled could only see a bleak future for themselves.

Our society has created a new generation of children that sound like they are in their seventies when they have yet to reach puberty. Small wonder when there are duck-and-cover drills in elementary schools in crime-ridden areas, when firearm deaths of children ages one through fourteen have totaled over ten thousand since 1979. It is a time when twelve-year-olds are saving money to buy coffins for themselves because their outlook is: "I never expect to become twenty-one."

However, this KidsPeace survey revealed hope as well as despair in the fact that almost all the children said their parents loved them (98 percent) and about two-thirds said they would go to their parents for advice on drugs, sex, and alcohol. They gave their parents good marks for best intentions but felt they were often not helpful role models.

In turn, with very few exceptions, parents love their children and want to help them grow up into strong, decent human beings capable of mastering life's problems. This chapter will detail the ways in which parents can empower themselves to be the secure, strong, competent role models their children wish for so they can guide them to a bright adult future.

• • •

## Authoritative Parenting

Parents are their own best authority about how to deal effectively with their children once they gain the skills of what we term Authoritative Parenting. Our concept of "authoritative" parenting is totally different from the old-fashioned, but still prevalent, concept of "authoritarian" parenting. To be "authoritarian" is, by dictionary definition, "one who demands absolute obedience, as against individual freedom." It is the approach of the parent who insists on obedience just because he/she is older, bigger, and provides economic support. It is the voice of authority that tells a child: "Do what I tell you because I'm telling it to you; you don't deserve any explanation since I'm bigger and older than you." It is the parent who believes punishment for its own sake will make a child behave, ignoring any mitigating circumstances. It is the parent who thinks in terms of black and white, always believing he/she is in the right. It is the parent who abdicates taking personal responsibility to educate his/her children to the right path in life, leaving that responsibility to the schools or justice system, organizations that have neither the resources nor abilities to act as parent surrogates, and then blames those organizations for failing to be of help.

On the other hand, an "authoritative" parent is "an accepted source of expert information or advice." An authoritative parent earns the respect of his/her children, rather than being entitled to that respect just because he/she is a parent. There is no honesty gap, no hypocrisy, because such a parent's words and deeds are identical. An authoritative parent, therefore, earns respect by being a positive role model, educating a child in what it means to be a secure, caring, responsible person capable of dealing constructively with problems, instead of running away from them.

It is even more important in a divorce than in a marriage to practice authoritative parenting. Both you and your ex-spouse need to reach agreement to do so in order to make your divorce a creative experience for your children as well as for the two of you.

Listed below are ten guidelines for practicing authoritative parenting that can help forge a lifetime connection of love and respect between you and your children. That bond will remain whether you remarry or stay single in the future.

• • •

## Ten Guidelines for Authoritative Parenting

### 1. Realize that you have more power to influence your children positively than you may think you have.

The most modern scientific data now demonstrate that parents exercise the most powerful influence on children's lives (television, peer pressure, and economic circumstances notwithstanding). The first three years of life, particularly, are of primary importance. This is the time when attachment is developed: A child's entire world consists of his/her parents in those earliest years. Consequently when a child experiences warmth, love, concern, tenderness, compassion, and kindness emanating from the small world of his/her parents, then he/she can grow up secure in the belief that the larger world is a place to develop one's abilities rather than a place to be feared. Attachment of this kind can be nourished throughout the duration of a parent-child relationship, building upon those early childhood years or correcting any attachment deficiencies of those years. As long as parents in their divorce love their children more than they think they hate each other, they can reach a mutual agreement to act in the best interests of their children even though they now are moving their own lives in separate directions. That means allowing equal time for both parents to nurture their children, agreed-upon adequate child support, and never using the children as weapons or spies on each other's activities.

### 2. Recognize that from the time of birth children are using you as a model for their own behavior.

Since you are your children's entire world in their earliest, most vulnerable years, they have a built-in sensitivity as to how to please you (or how to test the limits to which they can defy you in order to assert their own burgeoning individualities) in order to survive securely in the family household. As parents you are always being monitored by your children as they try to define how they are to behave now and in later years. This is known as parental imprinting. Your children are "inheriting" unconsciously the behavior you and your spouse are demonstrating as survival techniques, which they will replicate in their own lives. How you and your spouse's marriage works will provide the basis for your own children's ability to either cope with problems or experience helplessness in the face of adversity. There is an old folk tale, related by Simone de Beauvoir, that dramatically illustrates this reality:

> *A peasant makes his old father eat out of a small wooden trough, apart from the rest of the family: one day he finds his son fitting little boards*

*together. "It's for you when you are old" says the child. Straight-away the grandfather is given back his place at the family table.*

### 3. Cultivate empathy.

Parents have the power to understand their children to a far greater extent than they may realize once they use their empathy connection with their children. Empathy means sensitizing yourself to your children's behavior by remembering that you were once a child yourself and had the same feelings, fears, hopes, dreams, and problems your children have, even though they were acted out in a different time and place. It's well to remember your own fears of the dark, of aloneness, of abandonment, of being powerless in the face of bullies, as well as your anxiety over puberty changes, loving music your parents hated, wanting to become independent while at the same time desiring the security of family support.

On the other hand, sex as a life-threatening danger because of AIDS, drive-by shootings in school yards, the ever-present TV set (often called "the third parent") telling children you are what you buy and validating violence and irresponsible, loveless sex in prime-time entertainment (children born today will spend seven years of their lives looking at TV by the time they are sixty-five!)—all are anxiety-escalating events courtesy of modern times, so different from the times parents grew up in. However, contrary to conventional wisdom, childhood has always been a scary place to live in, where fears of abandonment, sexual anxieties, illness, accidents, and death were ubiquitous events, often unspoken but deeply felt. When you look at the sources of your children's fears, anxieties, and problems from the vantage point that you, too, once lived in the same dark places inside, you can validate your children's concerns and elicit from them the fears they try to hide so that you can help them deal constructively with those fears. You can empower your children to deal with their problems in ways that enable them to master them. Even if society infuses fear and helplessness in children, you can be the role model that demonstrates you *and* your children can make positive things happen in your lives by responding to fear with appropriate personal and social action.

In your divorce you can draw upon your inner resource of empathy for your children, who see the initial phase of parents living in separate households as a time of confusion, anxiety, and even terror. Understand their feelings of helplessness and insecurity. Encourage them to talk about those feelings. They might ask, "If you leave, will Mom (or Dad as the case may be) leave too, so I'll be all alone?" Or, "I'll be a good boy (or girl), so please don't leave." Or, "My friend Janey says she never sees her father after the divorce. Will I ever see you again?"

When you treat such concerns with the seriousness they deserve, you can reassure your children that you and your ex-spouse will always be their parents and will never leave. Living in two separate homes means two places your children can now live, not a separation from them. Grownups divorce each other, but never their children. Or, you can say it's very sad that Janey's father is not around, but you are different and *your* divorce means you still will always be present for your children. Above all, reassure your children they were in no way responsible for your divorce. Your children were always "good," and still are; divorce has nothing to do with it.

You can acknowledge to your children that the new situation is difficult, but that it will get much better as time goes by. So long as you communicate to them that you are in charge of the new situation and that there is nothing to fear and that your love for them will never disappear. When you are courageous, you give your children courage. But you must believe in yourself if you wish to have your children believe in you.

## 4. Bridge the parent-child love gap.

Parents and children show their love for each other in different ways. Often the gap between these two types of love can be great indeed. In our counseling practice we frequently hear men and women both tell us, "Yes, I know my mother and father both loved me. But my dad was never there for me even when he was home, and that was every night. He was always distracted, reading a paper, looking at TV, not saying much of anything at dinner except, 'How did school go today?'" We have seen men of fifty literally weep as they recall the fact that their parents (usually a father) never attended a single Little League game they were in. As for mothers, the complaints usually are, "She was always so critical, looking at my report card, pointing to the one B I got instead of the four As." Or, "My mom was so overprotective. I often felt I was living under glass. I always had to account for every minute of my life. I felt I just couldn't be myself."

Parents, on the other hand, would be amazed at these complaints: Don't they know everything we did for them was out of love? We were always concerned about our kids' welfare before everything else, and yet they took our behavior as being insensitive!

Being aware of the possible gap between your children's understanding of your love for them and their appreciation of you is an essential component of authoritative parenting. Enabling your children to feel they can express the widest range of their feelings and attitudes toward you without being condemned for doing so is the way in which this parent-child love gap can be bridged. Differing perceptions of how love is expressed can be acknowledged and understood and modified so that parent-child close bonding becomes a reality rather than a longed-for dream.

### 5. Cultivate the separate identity of each of your children.

Each of your children is unique in his or her own right. One may excel in school grades, another in sports or art. It's important to validate each competency in its own right rather than pitting one child against the other by saying, for example, to a daughter, "Why can't you get good grades like Susan does?" or to your son, "Why don't you take an interest like Billy does in basketball?" Instead, look for the gifts all children have that are unique to that child, and don't compare children's gifts, for they are all treasurable instead of being competitive. It's equally important never to criticize your children as persons. Listen to some mothers with a four- or five-year-old in tow at a supermarket and hear them say, "Toni, you stupid little girl, pick up that box that you dropped right now." The child's behavior needs to be corrected, but that has nothing to do with the child as a person. Calling a person "stupid" as if that person has a fatal character flaw is one of the most prevalent mistakes exasperated parents make. Said often enough to "correct" a child, it can have a devastating negative effect on that child's sense of self. Parents usually label children in this manner out of a feeling of frustration and are unaware of its potentially harmful effect. Parents can easily improve the way they correct a child by focusing on the child's behavior and saying instead, "Toni, your behavior is wrong. You know the rules: No touching items in the supermarket."

If, for example, a child, whose job it is to do the dishes, says, "But I don't want to do the dishes," a parent, instead of "losing it," can say, "I know you don't feel like doing the dishes, and I also realize that's a strong feeling in you, but sometimes we all have to do things we don't feel like doing. There are many times I don't feel like cooking dinner, but I do it anyway. There are lots of things people have to do when they don't feel like doing them. So, please do the dishes now." In this way, you validate the right of a child to express his/her feelings, but also firmly demand a change in behavior.

### 6. Cultivate spiritual and religious values in your children.

Authoritative parenting involves imbuing your children with spiritual values that will enrich their lives as long as they live. These values are best expressed by Dr. Benjamin Spock:

> *By spiritual values I mean any qualities or values that are simply not materialistic—not love of money or other possessions, although I appreciate and enjoy both, or love of power, which I enjoy too, but suspect.*
>
> *To me, spiritual values include the dependent love children have for their parents, parents' love for their children, and our love for people who show kindness. Spiritual values means loyalty to friends and relatives, dedication to causes and country, kindness to those in need, bravery and persistence, creativity and appreciation of the arts. For those who adhere to religion, it includes reverence for God.*

The potential for actualizing these values is inherent in every human being. Parents need to nurture the growth in themselves and their children if life is to become more than just sound, fury, and a drift to oblivion.

The generation inheriting the world today is the baby-boom generation—now going on fifty. It has reached that time in life when the widest variety of lifestyles have already been tested and found wanting; the self-centered ego trips of their twenties; the focus on careers, money, and social status in their thirties; the use of drugs and sexual promiscuity as pathetic attempts at self-enlightenment and as an illusory defense against growing older.

Now that their old saying, "Don't trust anyone over thirty," has become an absurd remembrance of the arrogance of youth, baby boomers in their forties and early fifties are beginning to learn to trust themselves. Life now becomes an affair of people rather than things; connectedness with one's children and one's own parents and friends are of paramount importance. It is this spiritual reaching out to others—to community, to a new love relationship, to remarriage—that is the vital component of a creative divorce.

The new concept of "character education" is spreading throughout school systems nationally. Courses in character education are being taught to millions of American children in the nation's public schools, to primary and secondary school students. The spiritual values outlined by Dr. Spock are included in this curriculum, and a special emphasis in this time of moral confusion and insensitivity is placed on "responsibility" and "respect"—respect for oneself as a caring person who can make positive things happen, and respect for adults who are role models and have earned the respect of children because of their actions as well as their words. The moral value of responsibility means being accountable by one's behavior and actions—being honest and truthful and living up to commitments, being self-determined and not running with the pack or bending to irresponsible peer pressure. An excellent example of this kind of character education as it relates to the question of when to have sex is enunciated by Professor Thomas Lickona, a leader of the Character Education Movement:

> *When you are engaged in this physical act, you are as physically close to another human being as you can be. You can't get any closer than that. When this is part of marriage, the sexual union is an expression of a larger union. The sexual love is a symbol or a sign of a marriage love. So you're joining your*

*bodies because you've joined your lives. You're giving yourself completely in the physical sense, because you've given yourself completely in the marriage commitment, so that the sexual union has a meaning of representing something that is much deeper, larger. Is this something you could not readily do on the first date or after you get to know the person a little bit better? Would it be as fitting with somebody you really didn't care about? Well, caring can certainly make it better.*

Emphasizing the seriousness, the spirituality of the sex act as Dr. Lickona does educates teenagers to refrain from sex without caring, sex without love, and unsafe sex. Taking responsibility for one's own sexual behavior means not responding to peer pressures or explaining away one's irresponsible sexual experiences because the use of drugs or alcohol "made me do it."

Parents in their thirties and forties and even fifties, needing a spiritual direction for their lives, are returning to religion and learning to appreciate the spiritual values inherent in all faiths.

They have lived long enough to come face-to-face with severe illness, accidents, and the death of family members or friends. At this point in their lives, they no longer view themselves as immortal, and the soul within them is crying out for a connectedness with a spiritual direction for the rest of their lives. Their children, who are hungry for a moral center in their own lives, are joining their parents in a commitment to a personal faith. Recent college educational surveys indicate that freshmen are signing up for classes, often oversubscribed, on the Good Life, Death and Dying, The Quest for Human Destiny, and the Bible in English Literature. Alexander Ashton, Director of UCLA's Higher Education Research Institute, recently summarized the results of his agency's survey of three hundred thousand incoming college freshmen: "Students are interested in things outside themselves, in society and community actions, in environmental concerns and helping people." Another educator, Jerry Gaff, in his independent survey reports: "There is a new emphasis on ethics and values, the effects of science and technology on society, love, and justice. This represents a big change from a decade ago."

These are the candles people are lighting instead of cursing the darkness of our times. Since divorce involves the death of a relationship, spiritual rebirth can become the consequence of that death. In a creative divorce we are stripped naked of our illusions and begin to understand the profound meaning of W.H. Auden's words: "We must love one another or die."

### 7. Recognize the truth in the African saying that it takes an entire village to raise a child in a healthy way.

Unless society at large (our African village) provides crime-free streets, high-quality schools with secure, nonviolent classrooms, an elimination of terrorism, and media that places a greater emphasis on caring, decency, compassion, and personal responsibility than it does on violence, crime, sex, lust, power, and cruelty, *all* children risk being damaged.

It also takes an entire village to destroy children's lives. Here is what Marian Wright Edelman, the outstanding children's advocate who is head of the famous Children's Defense Fund, recently said about our own society's relationship to children: "There are fifteen million children living in poverty in this country today. . . . No other industrialized nation has dreamed of letting its children go without basic levels of nutrition or medical care. When it comes to protecting our children, this is now an underdeveloped nation. . . ." (*The New Yorker*, January 15, 1996).

Authoritative parents don't drown themselves in helplessness and cynicism. They take personal responsibility to help change this state of affairs by participating in their community and church organizations and in political associations they believe can create a better life for children.

A creative divorce affords divorced men and women the opportunity to reach out in new ways that will enliven their lives, by making new friends, joining in church activities, exploring new job or career possibilities, or participating in environmental and human rights causes. You can become active in community programs such as crimewatch, get involved in school programs, participate in local elections, explore new interests (such as travel, theater, music, painting, architecture), make friends through the Internet (exchanging input from people in divorce who have similar problems and who can suggest solutions). We are fortunate to live in a society, flawed as it may be, where so many possibilities are available at minimum or no cost. Divorce is the time for grasping them. In enriching yourself you are also enriching your children's lives.

## 8. Be kinder to yourself as well as to your children.

Parenting has been called, with good reason, the "impossible profession." It is "impossible" because it can never be perfect. The perfect parent is a myth found in reel life rather than in real life. No matter how many books you read about doing the "right" thing for your children, real life itself will defeat many of the suggestions any book offers. This is not a sign of your failure to be a good parent but rather a recognition that parenting is a learning process for the parents as well as for the children, so that trial and error comes with the territory of raising children. We asked Elizabeth, who is forty-seven, divorced, and a mother of two grown children, what she learned from her children, and this was her answer:

"The children helped me grow up," she said. "They taught me what *responsibility* meant, that I could accept the duties and obligations of being a mother and could be depended upon to fulfill them, even after my painful divorce eight years ago when I had to return to school to start a new career. They taught me how to *listen*, not only to their voices but to their feelings and behavior also, how to hear what they were saying rather than what I would prefer to hear. They taught me *endurance*, *patience*, and *sacrifice*. They taught me I possessed *unsuspected strength* within me, which I discovered when I had to nurture them when I myself was sick. They taught me *empathy*, for in trying to understand them, I had to put myself in their place. They taught me *joy* in giving of myself because I saw my children prosper as healthy, intelligent persons as a result of my efforts. They taught me to think *independently* in the face of unforeseen illness and accidents when I had to make snap decisions on my own. They taught me that the *aliveness* and *curiosity* they possessed as children are two of the most valuable things in life, and I hope to have those qualities operate in me until I die. They taught me to *take risks in life*, not outrageous ones, but risks to obtain goals you might succeed in achieving if you stretched yourself just a little bit harder—like a child taking the risk of standing on two legs and trying to walk when all he or she knew before was how to crawl. Oh, I didn't know all this at the time my children were growing up. It's only now when you asked me this question that I realized how much I've learned from my daughter and my son. Maybe they ought to give me a diploma, since they were my teachers."

As parents, we can always welcome some words of reassurance regarding our relationship to our children. Here is what one wise man observed:

"Children today are tyrants. They contradict their parents, gobble their food, and tyrannize their teachers."

The man who said this was Socrates, and his words are over two thousand years old, proving that everything old is new again.

### 9. Teach your children to be honest.

Our friend Jane told us this story about her daughter Pamela that illustrates how children can learn to be honest:

One day Jane asked Pamela, when she was nine years old, if she would go to the store and buy a quart of milk because she was making a cake and needed the milk to complete the recipe. The neighborhood grocery store was only half a block away, and her daughter had many times before run to the store for something her family needed. Pamela went and returned with the quart of milk. Her mother noticed she was chewing some gum and asked her where she got it. Pamela said the store owner gave her a piece of gum, but when her mother questioned her again she started to cry and said, "I took it!"

Pamela's mother was horrified. She told her that what she did had a name and it was called stealing. Her mother sat her down and told her it was wrong to steal. She told Pamela to get her sweater on, that "we" were going back to the store to apologize to the store owner. Pamela screamed and yelled and refused to go back. Her mother looked her in the eyes and told her she must tell the store owner what she had done. Reluctantly, Pamela went back to the store with her mother.

Jane then told us: "The store owner heard Pamela's tale of regret and looked at me. I said I didn't want my child to steal and made her return the stolen merchandise. I paid the store owner for the pack of gum and left the opened pack on the counter. On the way home I said to my daughter, who was crying hysterically, 'Don't ever steal. People end up in prison by stealing. If you continue to do this you will be stealing everything you think you need, such as sweaters from department stores and other things. I don't want to visit my daughter in prison.' I also said, 'It was important you return the stolen gum. This act helps you, not me. Although it was difficult to do, you did it. I hope you never steal anything ever again. Yes, I said I do love you, but your behavior wasn't very good today.'"

Jane's child, Pamela, told her years later that she never forgot that incident, and she never stole anything again because it made such an impression on her.

Here's what we can learn from Jane's story:

1. Parents must be honest human beings themselves before they can teach their children about honesty.

2. Parents must teach children the value of honesty.

3. Nip bad behavior your child is demonstrating in the bud when it happens.

4. With love and caring, parents can instill decent family values in their children. Divorce need not be an obstacle to such character-building. In fact it can reinforce it by showing how a family overcomes problems rather than drowning in them.

### 10. If you are in a remarriage, practice authoritative *friendship* with your stepchildren.

Remarriage has become as American as apple pie: One out of every two marriages end in divorce, affecting one million children each year, and four out of five divorced men and women remarry. Remarriages are most likely to end in another divorce if the children are not dealt with skillfully. When remarried men and women are labeled step*parents* and the children labeled step*sons* and step*daughters*, false expectations and problems arise. These labels blind a couple to the fact that you, the stepparent, *are not another "parent."* These "stepchildren" have only two natural parents, and you cannot be a third. Children in almost every instance dearly love *both* of their natural parents, even though their parents are divorced and their mother and father may no longer like each other. Consequently, the most you can do to create a warm, loving, caring remarriage environment is to act like a good adult authoritative *friend*, rather than a parent, to the stepchildren. If you insist on being regarded as the "new" mom or dad, you create divided allegiances in the children, who feel they are put in the middle, forced to choose between their divorced parent who no longer lives with them and the new person they are living with. The children become resentful: they may like you but feel they are "betraying" their natural parent if they show that they care for you. They may then begin to exhibit their pain and confusion by acting out angrily or defiantly, causing great harm to the relationship. This need not occur if you inform these children the way one of our clients recently did. "Look," he told them, "I will never be your real father, but I can be a very good friend to you. Hopefully, you will want that to happen. You have only one father and I'm not taking his place. You can always see him and love him. So please always call your father "Dad" and me "Tom." I really like you and I love your mother. So let's see if we can get along as friends."

The children felt relieved. They no longer had divided allegiances. They were free to love their natural father and also free to like the new man, Tom, in their mother's life as a friend instead of a parent. They now are working out the problems in their new relationship skillfully rather than destructively.

There is also the need to remind yourself, if you and your ex-spouse are now living separately, that all households have rules that children must live by and each household differs in the kinds of rules that are set. Children of divorce are often confused about these rules. They may ask, "Why is it when I go over to Daddy's home he let's me do that, but here in Mom's house it's a no-no?" Explain to your child that different households have different rules. For example, when your child visits the little boy or girl next door, it's okay for those children to eat cake or cookies before dinner. But at your house it's not. If you educate your children to be tolerant of different rules in different households, it will help your child to grow up to be tolerant of different races and different people in the world.

Children in a remarriage also try to play the game of divided allegiance, such as going to Dad for a favor when his new wife has said no. Don't let your children break up a united front. It will support your children's own sense of security if they know you are together with your new partner in setting rules and discipline. Children often have difficulty adjusting to the new household and secretly want their natural parents to make up and still be married. The natural parents were the foundation of the child's life; giving up that foundation and adhering to the new household is difficult for children. But with empathy, kindness, love, and discipline based on caring and compassion, you can create a new, secure foundation for the children. Acting in this fashion, in the context of reinforcing the family values you and your new spouse believe in, will enable the friendship between you and your "stepchildren" to thrive.

• • •

## The Responsible Dad

It's hard to find a talk show that doesn't weep crocodile tears over the alleged heartlessness of divorced fathers toward their children. Fathers don't give a damn about their children once they divorce is the message the media projects as if it were truth revealed. But it is truth reviled! For nothing could be more false than the charge that most divorced men don't love their children.

In our long-term experience with counseling divorced fathers, we have heard hundreds of poignant tales about how much these men love their children yet are obstructed by the court system and/or an injustice-collecting ex-wife from having an ongoing loving relationship with their children. For example, there's the ex-wife who notifies her former spouse that Johnny caught a high-fever cold the day before he was to go with Dad on a week's vacation together and the father finds out later this was a lie. . . . Or the time when a father took a plane trip from where he lived two thousand miles from his former home to spend a three-day weekend with his daughter, only to find that his ex-wife had moved and failed to notify him of that fact. . . . Or the letter a father received from his ex-spouse saying their two daughters would not be allowed to see him again if he didn't send spousal support payments on time. This was said when he was downsized and was doing all he could to meet the support payments as best as he could. He was an honorable man, so this was not a ploy. All he needed was a bit of understanding until he could gain additional income. But that understanding wasn't forthcoming, so the children were held hostage to money payments.

We could give many other examples of how fathers have wanted to connect with their children but had barriers placed in their way. We have seen "strong" men weep in our office as they related how they missed their children and wanted to maintain a loving relationship with them.

There was a time, not so long ago, when men regarded themselves as second-class parents, for our society then programmed men to believe their only function at home was to bring in a good paycheck while their wives were in charge of nurturing the children. Indeed, I was a product of that time (until I learned better!) and believed my only function was to hand out cigars when my two daughters were born. After that the children primarily were my wife's concern.

Fortunately we've come a long way from that absurd relationship. In today's times, men take an active part in the birthing process and in caring for the children's physical welfare (many businesses now have bathrooms in which fathers can change a child's diapers). The father who bathes his children, reads to them, plays games with them, and puts them to bed is not the exception but the rule. They feel proud of doing so and delight in their interaction with their children. This is how the majority of today's fathers feel and act, and they wish to continue to relate in these ways to their children in their divorced state.

Yet the media keep relating the canard that men don't care about their children, and women writers continue to write absurd articles like the one by Susie Bright given great prominence in the Internet magazine *Salon*, titled "Who Needs Dad?" (11/3/97). Her answer was obvious: neither she nor the children needed a permanent man called "father" around. What she didn't do was survey the majority of children of divorce who would tell her, yes, they needed their dad and loved him and wanted to see him as frequently as possible. For every alleged "deadbeat dad" there are thousands of responsible fathers.

If you are a divorced father reading these pages, Pat and I suggest you eliminate the brainwashing you may have unconsciously incorporated in your own psyche that you are only a support payment to your ex-spouse and your children. Here are some ways that could help you maintain your role as a proud, responsible dad rather than a disposable one:

## The Seven Ways of Maintaining Your Role As a Proud Parent

### 1. Remember that both parents are forever.

Even if your ex-spouse remarries, that "stepparent" can never take your place as a father—all that he can be at best is a kind and caring friend since you are the only natural father they will ever have. Make sure your children are reminded of these facts. They will feel relieved that they are not put in the middle, that they don't have to "dislike" their father if they like their stepparent, or "dislike" their stepparent if they continue to love you.

### 2. Act like an authoritative (not authoritarian) parent.

Demonstrate by example that you can express your feelings and take charge of your new life without complaining. Show your children that they and you can acknowledge and learn from whatever mistakes you make instead of repeating them. You become a positive role model for your children when they see you productively active in your divorced life.

### 3. You always have a second chance to improve your relationship with your children.

You children will always love you and your ex-spouse no matter what happened when you were married. They will forget past difficulties when you acknowledge that you behaved unskillfully in the past but are now acting in a better way toward them. Make sure you put your money where your mouth is. Children have an endless capacity to forgive their parents' behavior when their parents become more attentive and loving toward them. They may feel depressed and show it by their lack of interest in friends, hobbies or school, or by getting failing grades instead of the good ones they used to get. By being alert to their problems, you can help them overcome them. When you are secure in your divorced life, they will feel secure.

### 4. Learn to respect and express your feelings.

We men have always been brainwashed to believe that we are not entitled to our feelings, that we are whiners or weaklings if we acknowledge that at times we might feel depressed, anxious, sad, fearful, or insecure. We need to eliminate this brainwashing and recognize that *all* feelings are neither good nor bad but are there inside you to be understood. Your children should feel free in your presence to express *all* of their feelings instead of thinking that you might not like them if they say they dislike something you are doing, or that you might punish them for "bad thoughts."

### 5. Don't use your children as spies on your ex-spouse.

Never ask them what your ex-spouse is doing when they are with her. Don't press them for information such as who she may be now dating, for they will feel they are betraying a trust. Above all else, they do not want to be put in the middle and will resent your placing them there.

### 6. Avoid continuing court battles trying to get even with your ex-spouse.

Solve the differences between you and your ex-spouse regarding such things as visitation rights, spousal support, and dealing with your children's behavior as reasonably as possible without the intervention of lawyers, who make money escalating such differences. Remember that both of you need to act in the best interests of your children since you both love them.

**7. Make certain you maintain your connection with the school your child attends.**

Tell the teachers and principal that even though you are now divorced, you wish to be treated equally with your ex-spouse with regard to being notified of all activities, events, and academic performance relating to your child. That includes notification of all open houses where parents are invited for discussions with their children's teachers. Don't automatically assume you are on the school's mailing list, for there is still a tendency of school systems throughout the country to ignore the father and relate solely to the mother when there is a divorce. For example, I have before me a survey sponsored by the prestigious National Association of Elementary School Principals titled "The Most Significant Minority: One-Parent Children in the Schools." As we have previously noted, "one-parent" is a misleading, false name for *two* parents who now are divorced and live in separate households. Responsible dads should make every effort to educate teachers and principals to the reality that fathers are equally concerned and involved with their children's school development as mothers. It is demeaning to a child as well as a father to be labeled a "one-parent" child.

• • •

Divorced parents are often confused and uncertain about how to cope with their own whirlwind of adult problems, let alone how to help their children overcome the difficult task of growing up.

Divorce *can* offer an opportunity to enhance your children's self-esteem, rather than have it be diminished by the process. Since children are receptive to any help their parents—the best role models possible—offer, and since parents want to provide the best possible upbringing for their children, new possibilities exist for bridging what we call the feelings-of-helplessness gap between parents and children. Both children and parents can benefit from the care, attention, and communication required by a truly creative divorce.

# 8

# DIVORCE, MATURITY, AND SELF-RENEWAL

Divorce in the middle years has now become a taken-for-granted fact of American life for the baby-boom generation. However, more often than not they see the Big Five-O, as so many boomers label their fiftieth year, as a threat rather than an opportunity for self-renewal. This generation of seventy-six million men and women are all rapidly approaching fifty. Unfortunately, they seem to have preserved their earlier belief that being young is "good" and being old is "bad." As if to confirm this, the *New York Times* recently ran an article that headlined the boomers' fear of aging—its title: "Kicking and Screaming, Baby Boomers Begin to Talk about Aging" (March 30, 1998). This kind of attitude can become a self-fulfilling prophecy for divorced baby boomers: if you consider fifty-plus "bad," you may give up on this chance to create a better life for yourself during these years even though you divorced because your marriage was intolerable. Without the opportunity for growth or change, your divorce may then become as much of a disaster as your former marriage.

However, your middle years can become a time for your self-renewal rather than a bleak end. It is of paramount importance that midlife divorced baby boomers understand the opportunity they're faced with, since self-renewal is an essential component of a creative divorce. If you are anticipating or going through a divorce in your middle years, you indeed face special challenges: confronting your aging process realistically, and dealing with your divorce as a knowledgeable mature person, rather than as an unskilled youngster.

We are fortunate to be living during an adult age revolution. This new consciousness of the opportunities available to mature people also reflects the fact that practically all of the frightening stories we have heard about aging being a disaster are false. Indeed, you can grow older *and* better if you empower yourself to learn about and act on the new realities of aging, which reveal that you can have an effective, creative, vital life after forty. (In the beginning of this century, people died—on average—at age 46!)

This chapter will detail this new reality—that these years can provide tremendous opportunities rather than despair for men and women who divorce at this point in their lives. Working at a creative divorce means recognizing and acting on these new opportunities for leading a fulfilling life, which can include new relationships of friendship and love.

• • •

## The Sound of the Aging Clock

"One day you wake up and find out it's ten years later!"

This is Gene, a divorced client, talking to us. He was turning fifty, being one of the first baby boomers born in 1948. He sounds shocked at his own words because he believed it wasn't supposed to turn out this way. "I thought I had all the time in the world to make it," he continued, "but it's all slipped away. I was forty only yesterday and now I'll be fifty, divorced five years ago and still supporting two kids."

Welcome to the baby boomers' middle years.

Gene has the common characteristics of people born in the earliest baby-boom years of 1946 to 1950: half of their marriages have ended, just like Gene's did; they have at least two children (like 69 percent of their peers); they have a mortgaged home (so do 78 percent of their peers); and more than half of the people born in these years are satisfied with neither their jobs nor their financial situation, and they don't believe they are in good physical shape.

It wasn't supposed to turn out this way, since they were supposed to be young forever and never trust anyone over thirty. In those heady days of nearly three decades ago *Time* chose the "Under-25 Generation" as its "Man of the Year" in 1967, proclaiming how fortunate these young men and women were since they were the most educated, most economically fortunate generation in American history. They are also the most powerful demographic group, shaping the destiny of America for generations to come because they make up almost one-third of the country's population—76 million out of a total 265 million.

They were singled out for glory. But now they find themselves singled out for possible unemployment because of business downsizing, singled out to be overworked, singled out for caring for their elderly parents who may suddenly be faced with heart attacks, strokes, Alzheimer's disease, or other adversities that often occur when one is seventy or eighty.

We live in an age-haunted society in which growing older has always been viewed as a fearful disease to be denied and disguised if at all possible. Gene demonstrates this, for he has dyed his hair to cover the grayness that would "expose" his age, and he tries to cover his bald spot, only half-concealing its presence. As Michael Lafavore, the 43-year-old editor of *Men's Health*, said: "Men have probably always been vain—you see those pictures of guys in the '30s and '40s with bad comb-overs. But baby boomers have taken it to a new level. They are convinced they don't have to age!"

But the reality of aging cannot be denied forever, for between January 1, 1996 and December 31, 2014, a member of the baby-boom generation will turn fifty an average of every 7.6 seconds. And after that milestone, these seventy-six million men and women will live an average of twenty-seven and thirty-two more years respectively.

Since the majority of separated and divorced men and women are members of this baby-boom generation, moving into their middle years coupled with the loss of their marital relationship can become terror-producing rather than being seen as an opportunity to create a better life. Hopelessness was what Gene initially felt about this situation. For if you believe that life is a downhill tumble into the grave once you turn forty or fifty, you will guarantee it to happen.

However, we are fortunate to be living in the time of an adult-age revolution, which can create *greater* opportunities for personal growth and happiness in the middle years than in one's earlier years. For divorced baby boomers, this can be a time for self-renewal rather than self-pity. Gene found this to be true; in continuing his story, we can observe how his expectations about aging changed from disaster into an opportunity to actualize new achievements in his middle years.

### The Power of Our Age Expectations

Gene was scaring himself half to death and asking for a future heart attack with his gloom-and-doom belief that his life was a downhill slide to nowhere now that he was turning fifty. Yet, objectively, he was a bright, intelligent man with an M.B.A. degree who had held a series of responsible middle-management jobs and was very successful. His weight had been normal and his health good—until recently he had been eating nutritious meals and limiting himself to no more than one drink an evening. But now he was turning flabby and new wrinkles around his eyes and mouth were beginning to appear. He viewed that as proof he was deteriorating because he was turning fifty. He subsequently learned that he was creating his own deterioration through a self-fulfilling prophecy: You get what you expect.

If you believe that being young is "good," that older is "bad," and that very old is ready for the garbage disposal, then you will live that belief.

In counseling, Gene was able to draw strength from his age rather than fear. It turned out he didn't like his job; a "nowhere job" was what he called it. But he had believed he was also a "nowhere man" because of his age. When he began to see he had transferable skills that could be utilized in a job he would like, he turned his attention to seeking out a better position. "Instead of waiting for the ax to fall, I used my current job as a steppingstone to find a new one," he told us later, after his counseling had ended. A lawyer friend was branching out his practice into the expanding health care field and was looking for the right person with extensive accounting experience to become a team member. Gene filled the bill since his special expertise was in the accounting field. He discovered fifty as a time for a new career beginning rather than an ending.

"It's the best career move I've ever made," he told us with spirited enthusiasm. He had made this happen as a result of the networking he did bringing him the offer of his lawyer friend. Knowing that he could make positive things happen in his working life had a ripple effect in his general attitude. He no longer saw himself as a victim because he was turning fifty but instead began to take personal responsibility to change his diet, work out, become less of a couch potato and more the man who was lovingly involved with his children again. "Yes, my mother's illness is an obligation, but instead of groaning about it as I used to, I'm taking it in stride. It's a burden, but one I gladly accept because she's my mom and I love her. I can never sacrifice as much for her as she did for me," he said. "And the kids are scholarship material, so they won't be drowning us in debt when they go to college. I don't think about my age like I used to; I wake up thinking more about the possibilities each day has to offer. And I'm dating again. A good woman is nice to have around."

Gene had to free himself from being victimized by the brainwashing society imprinted on the baby-boom generation that being young is the only thing that counts in life. Another very frequent kind of fear of growing older can result from a parent's negative experience with aging. We are reminded of Vincent, a 48-year-old man divorced seven years ago, who was already preparing for his own death since his father died prematurely.

### The Man in the Black Suit

Vincent had dramatically changed for the worse in the past year. He told us he'd been drinking too much, avoiding seeing his friends, and locking himself in his TV chair. He had become a TV news junkie, which he never was before, always looking at disaster stories—the bigger the disaster the better. He said he used to be quite active and was a good tennis player, but now his racquet is gathering dust. And his tastes have changed. All of a sudden he developed a passion for black suits and gray shirts while he previously favored bright colors. He had a physical checkup recently and told us he was given a clean bill of health but believes his doctor was shielding him from the truth that he had a bad heart.

It turned out that Vincent was suffering from a gigantic stereotype that he was unaware of until he discovered it in therapy. His father died of a heart attack at the age of fifty, and Vincent, now nearing forty-nine, was frightened that the same thing would happen to him. So he took what he thought were protective measures against the possibility of a heart attack. He thought inactivity and giving up tennis would strengthen his heart; he thought continuing to have an active sex life would bring on a heart attack. And unconsciously, he was preparing for death at fifty by wearing clothes fit for an undertaker, rather than the multi-colored clothes he so liked previously. His sad, sorrowful appearance and behavior, in fact, was a carbon copy of the way his father lived the last year of his life.

In our counseling sessions, Vincent became educated to the new realities of the aging process (e.g., sex is good for the heart; physical activity such as tennis makes one healthier; socializing with one's friends enhances one's will to live). Unconsciously, Vincent believed he was his father, so obviously he had to prepare himself for death. Once Vincent saw that none of his beliefs were warranted, that he was inflicting totally unnecessary pain and suffering on himself, he started to change back into the lively Vincent he once was. Yes, he still had some trepidation when he celebrated his fiftieth birthday, but he is now fifty-five, lively and gregarious, and plays a great game of tennis. He wasn't his father, after all.

We heard from Vincent recently. This is what he told us:

"You know, Mel and Pat, I was afraid to remarry after my divorce because I felt what's the use, I'll only die in a few years. Well, now that I'm over my age hang-up, I decided to marry again. I've always been in favor of marriage but felt I had married too young before. But now I met a great woman—she's 49—and we'll be married early next year. I never thought my fifties would be this great. I think my father would have wanted this for me. He'll be at my wedding in spirit."

• • •

## Redefining the Aging Process

Turning fifty is such a significant milestone in our society because of the huge size of the baby-boom generation. When one-third of our entire population will be fifty and over in the next eighteen years, attention must be paid to its profound impact on our family values, culture, politics, and economics. In fact, no aspect of our society will remain unaffected by the influence of this generation. One of the most profound impacts it will have is on our attitude toward the aging process.

This is the generation that sang about their anxiety and fear about not being needed at sixty-four, as if sixty-four was the absolute end of life. This is the generation that defiantly proclaimed that dying was preferable to growing old—by old they meant anyone over thirty.

On December 31, 1995, the day before the first of the baby boomers turned fifty, the *New York Times* drew extensive attention to this fact and wondered whether this youth-infatuated generation would accept, rather than deny, their aging process and see the possibility of new satisfactions in growing older.

There is hope for this turnaround take on the aging process in the very fact that the *New York Times* opened up this question for discussion. The dirty little secret fears about the aging process are now coming out into the open for discussion and re-evaluation. Indeed, the same rock stars who defiantly proclaimed that staying young was the only thing that mattered have themselves grown older and begun to redefine themselves in light of that fact. For example, the Peter Townshend who said he hoped he would die before he grew old is now over fifty! (He's one of the earliest baby boomers, born in 1945). He was an outspoken advocate of the "Me" generation, as the self-absorbed baby boomers were called. No, he hasn't died because he's so "old" today. Here are his thoughtful comments about who he is today in contrast to the eternal youth he once was:

> *I think growing up, maturing, is realizing that the pursuit of pleasure is usually a selfish pursuit. But it's very hard to pull yourself together and say to yourself, 'Hey, I've devoted my whole life to something selfish'. . . .*
>
> *Drinking became a problem for me when I used it to make myself feel good, when I had no right to feel good, or to run away from things I didn't want to face up to. One was the fact that I wasn't that tempestuous young guy anymore; I didn't need to be the center of attention at every party; I didn't want every girl that I saw; I didn't want to impress everybody. Drinking took me back to being adolescent and loathsome and the things that come*

> *up like natural armor. But actually it became a problem when I realized that I wasn't dealing with anything. Anything. I wasn't capable of sitting down with my wife and talking about the fact that we were becoming estranged. I didn't see the problem. I talked about other things. The booze. The band. But I never got around to straightening myself out and sitting down and looking her in the eye and saying, 'What has gone wrong?'*
>
> *I'm back with my family now. I'm growing up. We're all growing up. And that's not easy in rock-n-roll.*

Mick Jagger, now in his fifties and still leading The Rolling Stones, also is outspoken about his past and present attitudes toward age:

> *I've had a very interesting life, but you sometimes wonder how you'd have been if you'd been involved in something that would have expanded your brain a little more. . . . Everyone wants to be a star at least as soon as you get your first taste of it. You want to be well-known, you want to be on the cover of magazines. When you're twenty-one, this is what life is all about. That's kind of weird—it's not a normal or healthy attitude—but that's what I wanted. . . . It seems a little puerile now. What happens is you get very cynical very quickly. By the time you're twenty-nine or thirty years old you start to understand just a little bit about how idiotic you've been. . . .*

And Paul McCartney, who used to sing the worry of "Will you still need me, will you still feed me when I'm sixty-four," is now only a decade or so away from being sixty-four himself. In place of a typical rock and roll lifestyle, he became a devoted family man who was part of a long-term marriage (until the death of his wife).

There are many baby boomers who are thinking along the same lines as the rock stars quoted above. People like Peter Townshend, Mick Jagger, and Paul McCartney can serve as advance role models for aging baby boomers as they frankly share their changed attitudes about aging. If the baby boomers are willing to tap the positive abilities that inhere in their generation, they can overcome the negative conditioning they experienced about growing older and make the second half of their lives creative and productive, enjoying fulfilling family relationships that improve rather than deteriorate over time. For indeed, the baby-boom generation is the best-educated, liveliest, most mentally alert, physically healthy generation in American history. Indeed, this fact was not hype.

The past two decades have demonstrated high qualities of flexibility and innovation sparked by the baby boomers. If many of the innovations led to a dead end in those decades, current innovations, such as the concern for taking personal responsibility for one's health and returning to college for continuing education, are producing positive effects. What is most significant is that these men and women are cultivating flexibility and innovation in their lives. Their willingness to question received opinion, to take nothing for granted, to try new approaches when old approaches no longer work, are ageless qualities that they can exhibit in their later years. This baby-boom generation will not go gentle into that good night.

This capacity for being flexible, innovating, and risk-taking is evidenced in their approach to work and career horizons. They heard their parents tell them work was the main thing in life: have a nest egg so you'll be secure in your old age; stick to the same job all your life, even if you hate it. But inflation, recession, downsizing, and the presence of the information revolution have made a mockery of these injunctions. In this emerging information society, many jobs that were once considered lifetime occupations (particularly jobs in basic industries such as auto and steel) are now obsolete. However, many of these men and women are applying their ability to respond to new situations in a flexible and innovative way to this changed state of affairs. They see career changes as inevitable in this world, which is making established jobs become disposable tissues. Consequently, many of them have returned to college or are in retraining programs to enable them to become expert in new fields where jobs are available. They have become loyal to their own careers, rather than the companies that presently employ them.

• • •

## Taking Advantage of the Adult Age Revolution

It is a paradoxical fact that the members of the baby-boom generation, which has been the most age-obsessed generation in American history, have the greatest ability and opportunity to demonstrate that their chronological age need no longer define who they are and what they might become.

To do so, however, it is necessary to eliminate all the preconceived beliefs you might have about the meaning of chronological age and how "old" you presently are. For we are experiencing in today's times an adult-age revolution that is shattering all previous conceptions and expectations about how your chronological age "should" control your self-image, beliefs, attitudes, behavior, and expectations throughout your life.

Here are the components of this new view of the aging process:

- It views chronological age as only one identifier in our life. Who we are is not determined by how old we are.
- It views each person as a unique individual rather than as a captive in an age ghetto.
- It defines people in terms of the qualities they possess (such as curiosity, self-awareness, risk-taking potential, intelligence, sensitivity, empathy, flexibility, social concern, motivational drive, and personal responsibility) rather than by their chronological age.
- It views the aging process as an integral part of life. Just as we can enjoy each changing season, we can savor the changes the years bring. Growing older is an invitation to live more skillfully rather than a way station on the road to death.

This is an inherently optimistic view of the aging process instead of the hopeless view previous generations held about growing older. It is a scientific view derived from all of the new findings about aging and its meaning to our lives, which indicate that senility is *not* inevitable; that any loss of memory in older people is more related to depression than to any diminution of brain cells, which is minuscule in any case; that the ability to learn does *not* diminish with age; that there can be exciting sex after fifty; and that middle-age physical decline is more the result of what we have done and are doing to our bodies than what age has done to them, and that much of this decline is reversible.

• • •

## Learning to Be Yourself Rather Than Your Age

The first step in breaking the chronological age addiction and becoming who you are rather than just the number of your years is to complete the following sentences. Don't worry about your answers; those which come to mind first will be the most revealing and helpful to you:

1. The things about me that are *young* for my age are . . .

2. The things about me that are *old* for my age are . . .

If your answers are like those of the men and women in our seminars, they will fall into an easily recognizable pattern, without regard to the age of the respondents.

Typical of the attributes listed as "young" are:

- *Physical vigor*
- *Good health*
- *Flexibility*
- *Capacity to change*
- *Adventurous spirit*
- *Enthusiasm*
- *Optimism*
- *Willingness to take chances*
- *Zest for living*
- *Physical attractiveness*

Typical of the attributes listed as "old" are:

- *Lack of muscle tone*
- *Overweight*
- *Boredom*
- *Friendlessness*
- *Fears of rejection*
- *Rigidity*
- *Unsatisfactory sex life*
- *Illness*
- *Fear of the future*
- *Unhappiness*
- *Sensations of being trapped*
- *Loss of physical attractiveness*
- *Loss of memory*

Many people, when presented with the pattern in these responses, are blind to the implications they hold. "What is so striking?" is their reaction. "That's the way life is. You've got to learn to live with it." But consider the fact that these responses, which represent a sampling of hundreds of men and women from teenagers through senior citizens, are segregated more according to "positive" and "negative" than "young" or "old." Young equals good, old equals bad. And this equation seems to hold at virtually *every* age. One young woman said she wished she could change careers, but that she was "too old" to get the hang of a new job. Her age? Twenty-seven. A man complained, "My marriage, my kid, a nowhere job. I feel trapped. I guess I just fell into the easiest pattern at the time, and now I'm too old to change it." He was twenty-four years old.

As soon as they see this connection, the men and women in our seminars are quick to volunteer *negative* youthful qualities—"lack of self-confidence," for example, or "unclear goals," "inability to make decisions." They then listed *positive* qualities in growing older, such as "gaining wisdom," "the ability to accept oneself," "the experience necessary to shortcut a trial-and-error approach to life," and many others—including some that they first listed as "youthful."

This little test demonstrates the fallacy of ascribing the positive and negative characteristics in oneself to your chronological age. As one of our clients who took this test said, "I keep thinking of my cousin, Harold. He's sixteen, but I swear he was born seventy-five!"

The capacity to make positive things happen at any age is within your capability. But first you have to let yourself out of your chronological-age jail: you have the key, all you need to do is open the door.

• • •

## Being Fifty: A Time for Personal Growth

Role models are needed to enable us to break the harmful chronological age habit. We draw hope for our own future when we see men and women, not basically different from any of us, renew themselves, grow, and change for the better after fifty—proving wrong the old stereotype that programmed us to believe the fifties was the time for a down payment on a gravesite. Since we are now living longer and having children later in life, our children may still be young, and because they view us as role models on how to behave when they grow up, we need to assume personal responsibility to demonstrate to them that growing older and turning fifty is something to be welcomed rather than feared.

It is really important to look forward rather than backward. A lot of women try to look younger than their age by wearing more makeup. They sometimes wear extremely short dresses and skirts. Some women will keep the same hairstyle they wore when they were twenty or thirty. That hairstyle may have looked good on you when you were that age, but now it could be time for a change. Diet and exercise are important: eating sensibly and exercising twenty-five minutes three times a week can make you look terrific. Maybe it's time to experience a new wardrobe—something you might not have chosen before but admired in the stylishness of other women. A daughter will delight in seeing these changes, since they demonstrate her mother is trying her best at her age to act and feel as good as she can.

Based on your attitude, your children are receiving the message from you that fifty is going to be either terrific or frightening for them when they reach that age. What children need in those young years is a stable, happy mother doing the best she can at her age, and if children see you don't complain about your age or your divorce or your ex-spouse to them, then they will feel secure that mom seems happy with life today. What children need in those impressionable years is a mother getting on with her life, trying new and exciting things, rather than always complaining after her divorce about the terrible mistake she made by marrying "that father of yours." It's by example, the things you do, the way you behave, that children really learn.

Men, as well as women, can and do feel anxious and insecure about turning fifty and may experience a low sense of self-esteem. Since a son usually models himself after his father, it will have a negative impact if he sees him treat his mother without respect and love because he is feeling so insecure about his age. It is, therefore, equally important for a father to feel comfortable and maintain a high level of self-esteem when the fifties arrive. Paying attention to his grooming and physical shape, responding to being fifty as a challenge to make life more interesting and exciting, is the best gift divorced fathers as well as a divorced mothers can give their children and themselves. Your divorce is not a barrier to this development; it can alert you to the need to make this happen.

In our counseling practice, we have been fortunate to become acquainted with many of these men and women who searched out new horizons in their lives instead of making the excuse of their divorce and age as the reason their lives are so empty. Here are some examples:

- *Sharon*, fifty-one, used her menopause experience as a time for self-renewal, a time that occurred six years after her divorce: "I had quite a hard time with my menopause. I can remember being so emotional. I cried at the teeniest problem. My ex-husband used this excuse and my wrinkles because of my age to get a divorce. My teenagers were mad because I was so possessive and 'mothering' of them. And I was. I'd get into the car and follow them. I'd call and make sure they went where they said they were going. And I tell you, these were kids seventeen and eighteen years old. Finally my daughters talked me into going and seeing a doctor. Well, I did go to see the doctor who confirmed that I was going through menopause. He didn't tell me anything else. He didn't tell me why I felt so creepy. He just told me that he was going to put me on hormones and that they just put women on hormones to pamper us because we got so emotional over everything. It was so patronizing. I could have hit him! Now I look back at everything, and I've apologized to my children for being so overwrought all those years, which I thought was due to my divorce. Now, if anything, it's been a very sexually freeing experience. I've never felt so complete as a woman. I've formed a monogamous relationship with a great guy. We're living together, and we're talking about maybe marrying. It's good to know that's my free choice and not something I have to do, like my first marriage because my parents said I was becoming an old maid of twenty-five. Would you believe it?!"

- "Around fifty," *Ben* says, "I definitely went through a change. It wasn't physical, but it had a lot to do with my sense of self-worth. I felt that I was no longer the virile man I was at twenty and thirty. I really became aware of that. I left my wife and started really stretching my sexual 'legs.' I went through two years of this until one night while I was having my dinner, which consisted of peanut butter, cheese crackers, and coffee—I was too lazy to go out and get something and cook it, and I was tired of restaurants—I realized how lonely I was. None of the women I was seeing really turned me on mentally. It was all so empty. So I called my wife and started to court her again, and six months later she took me back. Sex now is not as important as it used to be. What matters are love, caring, sharing life together. I can remember thinking to myself that if I lost my ability to have sex, I wouldn't want to live anymore, but now there's so much more to life. I don't think it would matter much, but, thank God, I'm potent and my wife and I truly enjoy our orgasms!"

Ben's example indicates that when values change and there is enough love left and forgiveness takes place, an imperiled relationship can be improved rather than severed. Pat and I have seen this happen. However, it happens infrequently because too much injustice-collecting ends too many marriages long before a legal divorce takes place.

- *Jack*, fifty-five, who was divorced six years ago, told us how he took personal responsibility at fifty to transform himself physically. "I had high blood pressure. I was on medicine that had an adverse effect on my overall health. I was a workaholic and thirty pounds overweight, working sixteen hours a day, drinking and smoking, and on a course to a heart attack at fifty-five—if I made it to that. Four months and twenty-three days after my fiftieth birthday, I made a New Year's resolution to lose the weight. I played three sets of tennis the next morning and had to go to bed for the rest of the day. Two months later, I climbed on the scale and weighed two pounds more than I had on New Year's. I felt if I didn't do something now, there was no point in living. So I finally said, 'Get me to a fat farm.'

  "I went to a fitness resort where they gave me a diet and exercise plan. Cold turkey I stopped drinking and smoking. By the time I left, I had thrown away my blood pressure medicine and went from thirty percent to fifteen percent body fat. Thirty pounds lighter, I was on a natural high, better than liquor and cigarettes.

"I said then that I want to feel like this forever, and I do feel that way now, five years later, because I've kept the same health habits I learned there. I work at it. I learned in my business that there is no such thing as a free lunch, so why should it be any different when it comes to taking care of my health? Sure I work at it. I've also stopped working eighteen hours a day. I'm spending more time doing things I like—playing golf, gardening, seeing a good show. When I say I feel younger today than I did at fifty, or forty for that matter, I'm not kidding myself. I've more energy and am in far better shape than I was then. I was divorced six years ago—no kids, but our divorce was a horror. I'm happy with my life now and don't intend to marry again. Not my cup of tea, but some of my friends remarried. That's okay for them—my choice is my own, their choice is theirs.

- *Dewey*, fifty-one, divorced five years ago, transformed the imagined "loss" of his only son into a new purpose in life. Fortunately, he and his ex-wife had cooperated in never using their son as a weapon against each other. Here is what he told us:

  "Deep inside me I missed my son Terry, who had left to go to college in another state. He and I had always been so close, even after my divorce, for he was our only child. We played baseball together and his friends were my friends. Our bond was so great that I began to mourn his loss as soon as he left: I felt abandoned. I lost my interest in sex, I ate everything in sight and I gained forty pounds in three months. I was getting told at my work I'd better improve or else.

"I finally went to see my minister, and there I was talking with him and crying like a baby. My life is over, I said. All the joy and reason for living has gone out of my life.

"The minister listened intensely and then after I had finished, he said, 'You know, Dewey, sometimes God gives us special talents like your enjoying your son and his friends. God, I believe, gave you a gift.'

"'But Terry's gone,' I objected, 'and I miss him and all the activities we did together.' The minister said, 'Dewey, you've come to the right place. We at St. Thomas are looking for a person with your achievements to coach the teenage baseball team. And we also need someone to take these young men in hand. You would be surprised, Dewey, how many dads can't find time to watch their sons play sports. They are too busy working. But these fine young men need someone like you, Dewey, who enjoys working with young adults. I think you will do just fine. Would you be interested?'

"I took my minister's offer like a drowning man to a lifeboat, and then I began to establish a new routine for myself. When I came home from work, I coached the team from five to eight, three nights a week, and on Saturday I would be involved in the team's baseball games. I would also counsel troubled kids who were on the team."

In place of mourning the loss of his old relationship with his son, Dewey was establishing new connections.

And he discovered that in place of a parent–young child relationship with his son, he could establish an adult-to-adult relationship with his now grown-up son. Dewey once again became a happy man interested in life. He told us he's getting married to a divorced mother whose son is the shortstop on the baseball team he coaches. "I thought I'd never marry again after I divorced my wife Toni eight years ago. But as they say, you never know. I met Elaine two years ago and it was sparks between us from the very beginning. She's forty-nine and I'm fifty-one. We've got a lot of years ahead for us."

Dewey's experience is convincing proof that, contrary to conventional wisdom, men and women are from the same planet. The loss of a father's old relationship with his children can be as deeply painful as a mother's loss. He also learned—as many people his age have—that "never" is only a temporary word.

- *Rose* discovered it was never too late to adopt a child, which she did when she was forty-eight. Here is what she told us:

  "I ended my marriage to Hal because I wanted a child but he didn't, and it broke my heart. There was too much bitterness between us to stay together. It was too late to have my own child—I was forty-six when I left him, but it was better going it alone than being angry at each other all the time.

  "It then occurred to me to try to adopt. In these times that wouldn't be impossible just because I was living as a single person. I was a healthy woman with a good job managing a software supply house. While my divorce was painful, I didn't feel it was the end of the world. To the contrary, I felt that if I stayed in my marriage it would have been the end of the world for me. I did a lot of networking, and as luck would have it, my M.D. told me he knew of a baby being born to an unmarried mother who was giving the child up for adoption. Her only request was she wanted a mature, well-educated woman with a good job to adopt the baby. The fact that I was divorced did not change her mind after she met me in an interview.

"To make a long story short, Carrie, a beautiful baby, was placed in my care and I adopted her.

"I was kind of insecure about my age. Would I be able to be a good mother to Carrie, would I be able to do all the things a young mother could do quite easily? I kept fighting those fears about my age and before I knew it she was in kindergarten, then on to first, second, third, and fourth grade. But I still had doubts about being too old to have a child that young, and compared myself to younger mothers at PTA and parent conference meetings. I had the feeling that they must be better mothers because they are so much younger than me.

"But one day Carrie brought her friend Jill home from school. I made homemade cookies and chocolate milk for them and we all sat around the kitchen talking and laughing with each other. Carrie suggested she and Jill play a game she had in her bedroom. After I cleaned the kitchen, I went by Carrie's room to check to see if the girls were all right. The door as ajar and as I browsed by I heard Jill saying to Carrie, 'I wish I was your sister and lived here in this house with you and your mom. I think you have such a great mom. She looks like a mom ought to look and she is so nice and sweet and kind. You are so lucky, Carrie, because my mom isn't as nice as yours. She's always worrying about something, about how she looks or her weight.'

"My heart beat fast and I knew at last that my age had nothing to do with really loving and showing you love children. I'd really like to leave a message for mothers out there: don't let your age stop you from adopting children, no matter how old you are. Your life truly begins when a precious child comes into it. There is indeed a great feeling of completion for you. To care about another human being gives great satisfaction and the most happiness that I personally have ever known. And if you choose to be single, like I did, that shouldn't stop you."

• • •

## A Creative Divorce Means Making Friends with Your Age

We could multiply the examples we have cited many times over. These men and women are forerunners of the baby-boom generation's future: a future of productive middle-years activities, reaching out in new directions in a society that offers a great variety of choices for living well after divorce. It is evident that one need not be remarried, nor have children if one wishes not to. It's also acceptable in today's times to remain single and instead "marry" a spiritual or social objective, such as dedicating one's life to church activities or to a human rights cause. And living together without a marriage license is also acceptable if it is a monogamous, dedicated relationship. And sometimes a personal conflict over the nature of one's sexuality emerges in the later stages of a marriage and leads to a divorce. A person may discover he or she is bisexual or primarily gay and will then develop new same-sex relationships. These relationships can be and often are as loving, caring, monogamous, and committed as the best heterosexual relationships are. Our society is now more accepting of this reality, and the belief that such changes are a "disease" or "perverse" is disappearing as evidence mounts to indicate that sexual orientation is based primarily on genetic factors rather than the whim of personal choice.

Pat and I have also counseled many homosexual couples—gay men and lesbian women—to help them improve their "marriage" (yes, they are as committed to a loving, monogamous relationship as any heterosexual couple). They also experience the same painful stresses and strains when they "divorce." There really is no need for quotation marks around the words marriage and divorce if we focus on behavior rather than on legalistic terminology. We are all members of the human race, and as such nothing human can be alien to us.

With all the anxiety-provoking effects of living in today's time of transition from an industrial age to the age of the microchip, we can welcome the fact that we have become a far more tolerant society when it comes to personal choices in relationships. And these choices do not diminish after a divorce if one is moving into one's middle years. Indeed, the baby-boom generation needs to face the fact that they can no longer be young forever, as they once believed God had willed them to be. To substitute the reality that growing older is a natural process that can be utilized to enhance their lives rather than diminish them is the gift they can give themselves—a gift that enables them to build toward a future of positive achievements in place of regrets about the past.

The poet Tennyson's reflections on the aging process clues us in to our possibilities. Here is what he wrote:

*Ah, what shall I be at fifty*
*Should nature keep me alive,*
*If I find the world so bitter*
*When I am but twenty five.*

What Tennyson says applies at *any* age. Our attitude toward our chronological age and the way we behaved *before* reaching our present age creates our view of the world: Fear aging and you fear the world. However, we can change our view of ourselves and of our chronological age *at any time* in our lives. To change from fearing our chronological age is to triumph over hopelessness. The "bitterness" that Tennyson writes about can evaporate. The taste of life can become sweeter, and we can start tasting it at fifty.

# EPILOGUE: HOPE

Hope is the revitalizing power that generates a creative divorce; it is the hope that one can create a better future for oneself, and also wish the same for an ex-spouse, now that you journey in different directions.

Our book is our attempt to share with you the ways in which you can make positive things happen in the face of the traumatic events that inhere in the divorce process. The demon of defeatism that lurks in divorce can indeed be slain when you maintain the hope that indeed you have the ability to prevail over the adversities of divorce—and then translate that hope into positive action. Without such hope and action, the soul begins to corrode from self-pity, fear, and self-hate.

When divorced men and women come to see us for counseling, we always give them a copy of the following poem by our favorite poet, Emily Dickinson, as a reminder and reassurance that they can create a better life for themselves.

**Hope**

*Hope is the thing with feathers*
*That perches in the soul,*
*And sings the tune without the words,*
*And never stops at all.*
*And sweetest in the gale is heard;*
*And sore must be the storm*
*That could abash the little bird*
*That kept so many warm.*
*I've heard it in the chilliest land,*
*And on the strangest sea;*
*Yet, never, in extremity,*
*It asked a crumb of me.*

The "hope" in Emily Dickinson's poem is the precious survival gift we can give ourselves:

It is not a don't-worry-be-happy kind of hope.
It is not a whistling-in-the-dark kind of hope.
It is not a self-deceptive kind of hope.
It is not a denial-of-reality kind of hope.

It is, instead, realistic hope that recognizes the seriousness of a problem such as divorce, and at the same time enables you to tap the resources of intelligence and courage that inhere in yourself to overcome the shocks and disturbances that confront you. The smog of cynicism and helplessness evaporates as you prove to yourself that your divorce can become a new beginning instead of a disastrous end.

# INDEX

**W**

## A Note to the Reader:

The next step after reading a book whose ideas seem helpful, is to put those ideas into practice in one's own personal life. To help you in that endeavor, please feel free to contact us as follows:

Mel & Pat Krantzler, Directors
Creative Divorce, Love & Marriage Counseling Center
P.O. Box 6213
San Rafael, CA 94903-0213
Fax: (415) 472-0603